The Stuff of Fiction

The Stuff of Fiction
Advice on Craft

Douglas Bauer

Ann Arbor
THE UNIVERSITY OF MICHIGAN PRESS

I want to thank the students and my colleagues at the Bennington College Writing Seminars, where some of this material was originally offered in lecture form. My special gratitude goes to Liam Rector.

PN
3355
B29
2000

A CIP catalog record for this book is available from the British Library.

Library of Congress Cataloging-in-Publication Data

Bauer, Douglas.
   The stuff of fiction : advice on craft / Douglas Bauer.
     p. cm.
   Includes bibliographical references.
   ISBN 0-472-09733-4 (acid-free paper) — ISBN 0-472-06733-8 (pbk. : acid-free paper)
   1. Fiction—Authorship.   I. Title.
PN3355.B29   2000
808.3—dc21   00-09766

Grateful acknowledgment is made to the following journals and publishers for permission to reprint previously published material.

"Emergency," from JESUS' SON, by Denis Johnson. Copyright © 1992 by Denis Johnson. Reprinted by permission of Farrar, Straus and Giroux, LIC.

LEGS, by William Kennedy, copyright © 1975 by William Kennedy. Used by permission of Viking.

For David Lehman

Contents

1

Introduction

In recent years, certain critical examinations of fiction have had as their aim a form of aesthetic sabotage—to devalue, and even to make disappear, the writer who's created it. The ambition of this book is vigorously unsympathetic to that aim. Simply put, it is meant to be of practical use to writers, and to do so by assuming the point of view of someone at the task, engaged with the work, inside the effort to bring an invented world to life.

Any pragmatic discussion of the writing process threatens to demystify it, but a certain demystification is not only permissible, in some ways it is requisite for our purposes here. In saying this, I'm making a distinction between the doing of the work and its ultimate result, because I believe that if we begin to think of the activity itself—the daily sweaty business of making animate sentences—to be something all-mysterious and dependent on the whimsy of the muse, then we are apt to be cowed and defeated before we begin.

To an extent it is understandable why writing tends to be thought of in such exalted terms, something finally beyond our efforts to influence either its cooperation or its quality. (I especially understand it when I myself have finished a miserably unsuccessful day of work.) After all, the pulse of invention is a thing that comes purely from within ourselves. It is born of some fortuitous alignment of emotion and psyche that is as impalpable as it is powerful. We cannot see or feel or hear or smell its origin, yet it strives to offer up to readers transporting sensations of touch and sound and smell.

Nevertheless, it seems vital to remember that it is not the effort but the *result* of that effort, the fiction that emerges, that is and will always be inviolably mystical.

Throughout this book, I draw on the work of some marvelous writers to help crystallize and illustrate the various points I'm making. These frequent consultations only follow from the habit of, I dare say, every writer who regularly looks to published models for inspiration and assistance. The daily request for guidance also makes clear the peculiar relationship that a writer, as opposed to a reader, has with literature.

As pure readers, we are sublimely vulnerable to fiction's effect, so that when we encounter a passage in a story or a novel that takes us to our knees with its beauty and its brilliance, we might think to ourselves, "Wow. How in the world did he or she do *that?*" But this reaction, as evidenced by the clue in the inflection, is inspired less by a craftsman's curiosity than by sheer, awestruck admiration.

But we read differently as writers. We are not so much recipients as coparticipants of a kind, simultaneously confronting and digesting the fictional universe presented to us and all the while looking for clues to the handiwork. Encountering that same stunning passage with this assessing eye, we still feel, yes, first a quick shudder of awe, but it is one that does not linger and instead serves to trigger an ardent workaday curiosity that asks, "How in the world did he or she *do* that?" The emphasis of our amazement has shifted. It's no longer primarily on the object, the *that*, but on the process, the activity, the *do*-ing.

In other words, as writers, reading, we are blatant oppor-tunists. And when we wonder how another writer *did that*, we ask with every intention of finding out. Thus motivated, we proceed to roll up our sleeves and study the piece, the scene, the passage that has impressed us; we disassemble it, examin-ing its parts to see how they cue and complement one another.

This second way of reading is neither preferential nor even—to the degree that it makes the more direct reading experience difficult—desirable. But alas, for the serious writer, it is pretty much inevitable. As much as I would like to think that a writer, if he chooses, can freely set aside his ulterior interests and read with the avidity of childhood, I fear this is more nostalgic wish than possibility. For a writer, it is extremely hard when reading to fall heedless and headlong into a fictional world, to push away the craftsman's microscope and look up to find oneself elatedly, uncritically amid a cast of characters and their harkening dilemmas. I myself find that I have the best chance for this immersion when I am reading something from an earlier period, where the worlds and the language and the characters' behavior have a nearly insepara-ble unity, making them all more immune to isolated study, thanks to the adhering properties of anachronism.

But in this book, we must be able to take things apart. So, with one major and a few passing exceptions, I have used the work of contemporary writers, where, as I said, I find it easier to inspect the working parts. The major exception is Shake-speare, whose genius makes him perennially contemporary and therefore open to dismantling and analysis.

With*out* exception, the standard applied in including cer-tain excerpts was as simple as it was foolproof: I love the writer and the work. Indeed, I did not so much choose as reflexively turn to these particular writers, whom I regularly reach for, and who have never failed to instruct me.

It should go without saying that in gathering together a

small number of writers, I am not implying any kind of hierarchy. There are of course dozens, hundreds, of others who could serve brilliantly as models. Offering, for instance, excerpts from Denis Johnson's story "Emergency" says only—nothing more, nothing less—that I know and love the story and have thought about the way it works.

In many instances—"Emergency" is just one of them—a piece of work has been called upon to do double and even triple duty, studied, say, in the chapter on characters, called back again to make a point about "High Events." This seemed only logical, since it is likely that if we really love a writer, we are drawn to the *whole* of his or her work, not just one aspect of it.

It also speaks once more to the difference between reading with no other motive but a love of literature, and reading dually as writers who are always poised to plunder. In the former case, one is naturally inclined to want to read as widely as possible with the constant hope of making new discoveries. The writer, though, reading to learn, can also profit greatly from reading narrowly and deeply. Reading, that is, all of one writer's work—or the works of a few writers with similar qualities and tendencies—for which one has an especially keen appreciation. And then reading them again, and again, attending first to the way characters are drawn, next for the patterns and cadences of the characters' speech. And so on.

There's a statement, generally attributed to E. B. White, that takes a dim view of this whole business. It speaks specifically to the notion of analyzing how humor works and observes that trying to do so is about as easy as dissecting a live frog, and that, *like* dissecting a live frog, the more determinedly one attempts it the more likely it is the thing will die in the process.

Yes, of course. But when a frog is dead, it's, well, dead.

Unless you believe that its essence is transported to another realm. While fiction—a wonderful story or novel—is capable of infinite resuscitations. After coldly, ruthlessly, dissecting it, all you have to do to bring it back to life is read it again.

I remember an essay by Harry Crews in which he recalls his own feverish, autodidactic apprenticeship. In it, he describes falling in love with Graham Greene's *The End of the Affair,* a passion that reached such a pitch that he literally took his copy of the book apart, tearing out its pages and spreading them on the floor and walking among them in order to try to understand the novel's structure. That, in effect, is what I am doing in this book, and I invite you to bend down, look close, as you walk around among the passages of some stories and novels that have been virtually taken apart and spread out on the floor. It is in the spirit of that ferocity, of Crews's obsessed determination, that we might all be inspired to learn continuously about the craft.

2

Openings

Ways of Starting the Story

The Grimms' fairy tale "Faithful John" opens thusly:

> An old king fell sick; and when he found his end drawing
> near, he said, "Let Faithful John come to me." Now Faith-
> ful John was the servant that he was fondest of, and was so
> called because he had been true to his master all his life
> long. Then when he came to the bed-side, the king said,
> "My Faithful John, I feel that my end draws nigh and I have
> now no cares save for my son, who is still young, and stands
> in need of good counsel . . ."

This beginning, altogether typical in form and strategy of
the tale or fable, strikes a tone of careful consideration for the
reader. Written with an audience of children in mind, the
story-setting information is naturally parceled out at a pace
and in a sequence that can be readily absorbed. You can almost
envision the teller softly clearing his throat, waiting for the
reader to be seated and comfortable and to indicate he's alert
to receive the story.

So, in "Faithful John," the reader first learns that there was
a king. Next, that this king was old. Then, that at his

advanced age he has fallen ill, acutely ill, so ill that he senses it is his final sickness. And so on.

As I said, there is a rhythmically processive quality to the prose. There are no allusive tidbits dropped to tantalize a reader. There is no immediate alarm or frenzied rush to startle and catch a reader's attention. There is only the steady, unruffled commencement of a tale, and the whole source of its power is the singularity of the story. Its ability to engage readers' interest derives purely from the degree to which they find the information incrementally more intriguing.

Now look at an altered first sentence of this opening:

When the old king fell sick and found his end drawing near, he said, "Let Faithful John come to me." Now Faithful John was the servant that he was fondest of and was so called because he had been true to his master all his life long . . .

Simply by changing the article, from "*an* old king" to "*the* old king," a significantly different tone is established. Rather than assuming, elementally, that the reader must first be made aware of his very *existence*, there is a suggestion, in calling him *the* old king, of a greater familiarity with the story and with those who populate it. A familiarity, that is, on the part of the *teller*. And this more casual knowledge carries with it an implicit message that the narrative is in this case less concerned about the reader's being patiently brought along. In other words, it is obvious the tale teller understands very well who he is talking about—"You know, the *king*"— and if the reader's initial nanosecond of response is to say, in effect, "King? *What* king?" the disposition of this narrator is, to a real degree—*I don't want to have to start from the very beginning just to get you up to speed. If you pay attention, it will all become clear.*

Further, there is a sense of quickened pace, emphasized by connecting the first two sentences with "and" to make one. The quickened effect is made, even more, by the addition of the opening word, "When," which implies that the teller has been discussing the king in his healthier years *before* the reader has arrived within earshot to pick up the story . . . *when he fell sick*.

Here is another alteration, a rearrangement, taking a sentence from the body of the opening paragraph and making it the first one:

> When he came to the bed-side, the king said, "My Faithful John, I feel that my end draws nigh." Now Faithful John was the servant that he was fondest of and was so called because he had been true to his master all his life long . . .

That sense of responsibility for the reader's understanding which characterizes the tale's actual opening has now been even further abdicated, and, as a result, readers must work still harder to make sense of the universe they have come upon. "Who's 'he'?" a reader asks. And again, "*What* king?" And, "Is Faithful John the 'he,' as it would seem?" Et cetera, et cetera.

Finally, this revised opening of the fair tale:

> In the years to come, when he sat with the young queen, whose life he had saved, and with her watched her beloved children, whose lives she had been willing to sacrifice to save him, he would frequently remember the day the sick old king called him to his bed-side and said, "My Faithful John, I feel that my end draws nigh."

In this instance, as the narrator foretells some of the tale's seminal events, an interesting kind of hybrid effect is created. Readers feel at once somewhat confused but also calm. It is plain to see why they feel disoriented, even more so than they have in the preceding two examples. After all, every bit of information in every sentence comes to them unexplained and out of any reassuringly sequential context. They are tossed about in time, immediately thrown into a future with people they have not really met, then back to a past to confront some dying old king. They cannot know what connects all this seemingly random information: once more there is a floating, unidentified "he"; there is a young queen who for some reason owes "him" her life; there are her children, whom she supposedly loves and yet, unfathomably, was willing to sacrifice for "him"; then there is the old king, who calls "him" by name so that the reader can at least know who "he" is.

And yet, for all the dislocation, readers do not feel quite the haste to orient themselves as they do in the previous example. Because this opening also indicates, as with the actual beginning of "Faithful John," that they are in thoughtful hands. Why? Well, in part, because the narrative has once again slowed to a pace similar to that of the Grimms'. Second, although allusions to some clearly important episodes are presented in reverse chronological order, there comes with that the impression of a thought-through pattern or narrative plan. Also, such foretelling creates a uniquely authoritative tone, a sense that the teller knows and has digested the full run of events and has decided to offer them in a particular order after having witnessed them, or heard them, to their end. Which means, therefore, that he is now standing at some distance from them, able to survey and arrange them from a commanding point of vantage.

At first glance, you might think that opening a story in this way contradicts a fundamental rhetorical strategy for attracting and holding a reader. After all, the ending, the result, has been given away in the first sentence. But in fact such a method of beginning produces a very strong curiosity in readers, as they immediately form the question, not, *What* happens? but rather, *How* did whatever they have been told happens happen?

Gabriel García Márquez begins *Chronicle of a Death Foretold*, not surprisingly, given its title, with this sort of opening: "On the day they were going to kill him, Santiago Nasar got up at five-thirty in the morning to wait for the boat the bishop was coming on." Even more famously, he starts the epical *One Hundred Years of Solitude* with these lines: "Many years later, when he faced the firing squad, Colonel Aureliano Buendia was to remember that distant afternoon when his father took him to discover ice." Note the movement, the compressed excursion through time on which readers are taken, in just this first sentence: from a starting point in the past tense, the narrative forecasts a *future* moment in which the colonel remembers an even *earlier* past than that from which the story is being told. With a manipulation of such deftness, it is clear there is a tale teller here who can masterfully juggle the chronological balls. And sensing this, we are inclined to give over instantly, trustingly, unguardedly, to the overarching vision suggested by such a voice.

It should go without saying that these four ways of opening a story—and here, as always, I mean "story" to include the novel as well—are by no means inclusive. Within them there are countless fine distinctions and subcategories. I immediately think, for example, of such opening sentences as *Pride and Prejudice*'s "It is a truth universally acknowledged that a single man in possession of a good fortune must be in want of a wife." Or Tolstoy's "All happy families are alike; each unhappy family is unhappy in it own way." Or, in contemporary literature, from *A Bend in the River*, V. S. Naipaul's bleakly admonitory, "The world is what it is. A man who is nothing, who allows himself to become nothing, has no place in it." These three beginnings, and their like, seem to me to contain aspects of both the opening foretold and also of the fable's reader-friendly "Once upon a time . . ." They suggest a narrator who has pondered the entire tale and, from an analytical distance, with its outcome in mind, has refined its meaning to an opening epigram, a preface of sorts, designed in part to brief the reader in a codified way on what is thematically to come.

Thinking generally about the opening of a story, I am not so much interested in any precise *unit*—the opening sentence, or the opening paragraph. I have in mind the less exact and more visceral matter of a work's introductory impact. Its announcing impression. The sound of its first chord and the response that chord produces in a listener, a reader.

Obviously, no one strategy is inherently preferable to another, since writers always seek to find a way of beginning which produces the *effect* they wish to establish, one that is peculiar to an individual piece of work. And it is that idea I want to examine here—the *characteristics* of various openings that determine their effect, the tenor they create; the ways they regard and stand in relation to their readers.

As the models we have just looked at show, an essential difference among various openings is the degree of effort, for lack of a better word, readers must bring to the task of immediately sorting out the landscape and the stakes—in short, the terms of the story. As we have seen, this effort (which should not imply a chore or a task; if the opening is effective the readers' so-called effort will be eager and go unnoticed) varies considerably, depending on how plainly and procedurally the writer chooses to inform them.

To extend the point with metaphor, the populated world of a story or a novel can be equated to a gathering of people in a room, whether it is a spirited crowd of revelers—imagine, say, a large and festive company Christmas party taking place in a chandeliered ballroom—or a single hapless exile brooding in a garret. And the reader who takes up a story can be thought of as a person opening the door to the goings-on—maybe mass celebration; maybe a misanthrope's isolated rue.

The question, then, for the writer is always the *manner* in which you wish your readers to gain entrance.

You might decide you want your narrator to, in effect, meet the readers as they are about to enter. "Now," your narrator says, stepping forward to intercept them, "let me tell you what's on the other side of that door. There's a large company Christmas party, Hybertext Software, and you know these high-tech geeks, working eighty hours a week and desperate for a little R and R. So everybody's getting good and juiced. Oh, and there's a scene by the bar you might want to check out. A guy's got a midget dog concealed in a straw basket, and he and his girl friend—you can't miss her, she's got a nose ring the size of a handcuff—seem to think it's all hilarious. Weird. Okay? Here we go."

Here, as in the actual opening of the Grimm fairy tale, the arriving guests at the party, that is, the readers, begin with a sense that they have been thoughtfully prepared for what they are about to encounter, thanks to the thoroughly apprising narrator. It is a way of beginning that serves especially well if the writer, however subtly echoing the fairy-tale prototype, wishes to establish a kind of mythic or fabulous tone.

Toni Morrison, for example, opens her novel *Sula* with a marvelous overseer's majesty of tone, one that almost begs for the first sentence to begin, "Once upon a time . . ." (Though Morrison, one of the last writers on earth to whom the term "formulaic" could be applied, of course refuses the invitation.)

In that place, where they tore the nightshade and black-berry patches from their roots to make room for the

Medallion City Golf Course, there was once a neighborhood. It stood in the hills above the valley town of Medallion and spread all the way to the river. It is called the suburbs now, but when black people lived there it was called the Bottom.

And Marilynne Robinson opens her novel *Housekeeping* in similar fashion, to similarly evocative effect, its first sentence artfully resonant of Melville's Ishmael.

My name is Ruth. I grew up with my younger sister, Lucille, under the care of my grandmother, Mrs. Sylvia Foster, and when she died, of her sisters-in-law, Misses Lily and Nona Foster, and when they fled, of her daughter, Mrs. Sylvia Fisher. Through all these generations of elders we lived in one house, my grandmother's house, built for her by her husband, Edmund Foster, who escaped this world years before I entered it.

Clearly, the features that define a fable's opening are equally apparent in these of Morrison and Robinson: the judicious distribution of the information; a direct and thorough and unhurried pace; all the elements suggesting a boldly unadorned wish to give readers a picture of the fictional world, the room, they are entering.

We saw, however, in the first altered opening of "Helpful John," that there are times when the narrator provides less custodial help. This is to say that you as the writer might wish for any number of valid reasons to let a reader pass through the door more or less unprepared. Perhaps the reader enters— without having first been intercepted and briefed—and immediately confronts a cluster of people surrounding someone who is in the midst of telling a joke. Perhaps, upon entering, the reader catches a passing streak of a man chasing a woman up the stairs to the mezzanine. Maybe, after stepping into the room, a reader hears two women engaged in a heated argument where they stand just to the left of the door. The point, of course, whatever the moment that captures readers' attentions, is that the action is under way and maybe moving quickly.

This impression of preexisting activity is key. As I said earlier, the most successful openings of this type give off the sense of an already running energy, one that has begun *before* the reader enters the room. Readers feel that they are joining behavior in progress, that the festive party has been going on without them, or that the misanthrope's solitary brooding has begun sometime before the moment when they open the garret door.

There is a splendid instance of such an opening in William Kennedy's novel *Legs*—which we will inspect more closely in the "Dialogue" chapter—where readers are immediately thrust into the middle, and must quickly make sense, of a lively conversation. Part reminiscence, part tall tale, part ghost story, it takes place among old drinking comrades. They are speaking of the murder of the gangster Legs Diamond, who has achieved since his death a stature of mythic affection in their minds:

> "I really don't think he's dead," I said to my three very old friends.
>
> "You what?" said Packy Delaney, dropsical now, and with only four teeth left . . .
>
> "He don't mean it," Flossie said, dragging on and then stubbing out another in her chain of smokes, washing the fumes down with muscatel . . .
>
> Tipper Kelley eyed me and knew I was serious.

"He means it all right," said Tipper, still the dap news-
man, but in a 1948 double-breasted. "But of course he's full
of what they call the old bully-bull-bullshit because I was
there. You *know* I was there, Delaney."

"Don't I know it," said the Pack.

"Me and Bones McDowell," said the Tip. "Bones sat on
his chest."

"We know the rest," said Packy.

This is exactly the sort of slightly disorienting opening
that, as I said, creates an immediate curiosity. Readers, upon
entering Kennedy's dark and historically malodorous Albany
bar, catch a provocative conversational snippet, and they want
to find out what is going on in there.

The seductive confusion that Kennedy accomplishes with
people talking is achieved in another way by Alice McDermott, in the opening of her novel *That Night*. Here, the reader
happens without warning on a moment of *physical* rather than
verbal motion:

That night, when he came to claim her, he stood on the
short lawn before her house, his knees bent, his fists driven
into his thighs, and bellowed her name with such passion
that even the friends who surrounded him, who had come
to support him, to drag her from the house, to murder her
family if they had to, let the chains they carried go limp in
their hands. Even the men from our neighborhood, in
Bermuda shorts or chinos, white T-shirts and gray suit
pants, with baseball bats and snow shovels held before
them like rifles, even they paused in their rush to protect
her: the good and the bad—the black-jacketed boys and
the fathers in their light summer clothes—startled for that
one moment before the fighting began by the terrible,
piercing sound of his call.

Again, readers presented with such an animated opening cannot help but feel they have been walking down a quiet, Long Island tract-house street in the summer, in the 1950s, and have turned a corner to witness this most unlikely brawl about to start. And though they have discovered it just a split second before the boys and the husbands launch themselves at one another, the scene has clearly already begun. Rick, the lovesick teenager who is pounding his fists into his thighs as he shouts his girlfriend's name, has *already* left the car and walked across the lawn to the front door of her house. The men of the neighborhood have *already* chosen their improvised weapons and have started across the street toward Rick and his friends. So readers inevitably and unconsciously get the sense that the action has commenced before they came along.

I won't belabor the discussion with unneeded analysis of other even more "confused" openings; openings where the readers find themselves squarely in the middle of the ballroom party, not quite sure how they got through the door, as strangers and their voices swirl around them.

But for example, here is the opening of Denis Johnson's story "Car Crash While Hitchhiking," from his collection *Jesus' Son:*

> A salesman who shared his liquor and steered while sleeping . . . A Cherokee filled with bourbon . . . A VW no more than a bubble of hashish fumes, captained by a college student . . .
>
> And a family from Marshalltown who headonned and killed forever a man driving west out of Bethany, Missouri . . .

And of course, there's the inimitable opening of *The Sound and the Fury:*

Through the fence, between the curling flower spaces, I could see them hitting. They were coming toward where the flag was and I went along the fence. Luster was hunting in the grass by the flower tree. They took the flag out, and they were hitting.

Surely, point made. In Faulkner's opening, readers are asked, without warning or preparation, to make sense of a physical world they are observing from *inside* the consciousness of Benjy, the idiot. It is a limitation of understanding and perception, a diction of distillation, that, in Faulkner's hands, achieves poetry's essential plainness.

Amos Oz, in his book *The Story Begins*, calls these initial meetings between a reader and a fictional world "opening contracts." It is a felicitous phrase, with all its implications of encounter and commitment and partnership. Oz goes on, examining in the course of the book ten eclectically chosen works, to address such issues as the credibility of the narrator, the sometimes apparent but false pact between writer and reader, and other subtleties of rhetoric that I will touch on in later chapters but am less concerned with now as we more narrowly ponder the nature and power of an opening's lure.

Oz also cites a very useful distinction, made by Edward Said in *Beginnings: Intentions and Methods*, between "origin" and "beginning." According to Oz, Said regards "origin" as a "passive" concept, one belonging to the divine, whereas "beginnings" are "active," are matters of history and, says Oz, always include both "intention and attitude. Every beginning creates uniqueness but also weaves [in] the existing, the known."

Appropriating these two terms for our purposes, it seems to me we could think of origin as a realm belonging to the writer, alone, in the stages of conception and composition, as he or she is living with the raw material. Origin, then, is that time and place in his or her imagination where the writer is inventing and shaping the world and the people who will be ultimately unveiled.

After that there comes beginning, the active, vibrant moment when the writer *does* do the unveiling, presenting his or her now aesthetically ordered origin to the reader; when a calculated energy draws the reader in; when, that is to say, the door to the room of story is at last thrown open to the public.

In considering possibilities for opening, for beginning, we have seen that it can be extremely appealing to readers to have a fictional world somewhat laid out and panoramically depicted for them before they encounter it. If described with sufficient allure and appeal, they will be unhesitantly eager to enter.

And it can be just as riveting for them to find themselves instantly, somewhat uncomprehendingly, in the midst of some confusion, mild to considerable, if the snatches they receive as they are getting their bearings are made provocative and arresting.

But as we think about these differences and distinctions among openings, we should above all keep in mind that most fundamental assignment that they all have in common: to beckon readers; to seduce them; snare them; draw them in. "Readers," said Ted Solotaroff, "are a group of people waiting to be interested, which is within their right."

So readers are willing, amply curious to hear a writer's tales, a fact they continue to demonstrate, God bless them, by their simple gesture of turning to them with a sense of anticipation.

And then they wait to see, which is, as Solotaroff correctly says, within their right.

Finally, I offer two more openings that I love, the first from Edmund Wilson's story, "The Old Stone House":

As I go north for the first time in years, in the slow, the constantly stopping, milk train—which carries passengers only
in the back part of the hind car and has an old stove to heat
it in winter—I look out through the dirt-yellowed double
pane and remember how once, as a child, I used to feel
thwarted in summer till I had got the windows open and
there was nothing between me and the widening pastures,
the great boulders, the black and white cattle, the rivers,
stony and thin, the lone elms like feather-dusters, the high
air which sharpens all outlines, makes all colors so breath-
takingly vivid, in the clear light of late afternoon.

Like all great openings, like all of those I have referred to
here, Wilson's only demonstrates that the best of them elude
strict and narrow categorization. Is this an opening articulated
with a fable's conscientiousness? To some degree, certainly, as,
with a rhythm of language at once both lulling and stirring, it
depicts the sweep of physical landscape and hints, as well, of
Wilson's interior one. But doesn't this passage also, to an
extent, assume the reader is already on board, since the explanation of the ride and its destination comes, not before, but
only in the *course* of the train moving north? And doesn't it,
too, ease us back and forth in time, not foretelling, but sensa-
tionally recalling? I think it does a bit of all these things.

And lastly, this opening, the beginning of chapter 13 of
E. B. White's *Stuart Little*:

In the loveliest town of all, where the houses were white
and high and the elm trees were green and higher than the
houses, where the front yards were wide and pleasant and
the back yards were bushy and worth finding out about,
where the streets sloped down to the stream and the stream
flowed quietly under the bridge, where the lawns ended in
orchards and the orchards ended in fields and the fields

ended in pastures and the pastures climbed the hill and disappeared over the top toward the wonderful wide sky, in
this loveliest of all towns Stuart stopped to get a drink of
sarsaparilla.

Among the many things to admire in this opening, I will
point out two—first, the quick nod, the beguiling reference
the narrative makes in the midst of its unimpeded and imper-
turbable flow, to the backyards, which are for some reason
"worth finding out about." And second, the abrupt concreteness of the sentence's finish, an endstop of elegant impact, its
velocity concluding in a funny and most apposite image of a
mouse on a voyage in need of a drink.

You can almost physically feel the pull, the graceful muscle
of White's opening, as it draws readers into the room and
fluidly moves them across its entire breadth, gliding past all the
occupants, until they stand at the bar at the other end with
drinks, perhaps sarsaparillas, in their hands.

It is that sort of pull, with that insinuated strength, which
writers should always try to achieve in opening their stories.
Openings with the ambition to take their readers into states of
alert yet childlike intrigue, making them the kind of ingenuous
readers the brothers Grimm had in mind.

3

Dialogue

The Reader as Eavesdropper

The best lesson I ever received on the nature and function of dialogue came as the result of a magazine assignment. I was asked—this was more than twenty years ago—to write a profile of a fascinating man named John Maher. Maher lived in San Francisco and had started an organization called Delancey Street to help alcoholics, addicts, and ex-convicts find their way back to lawful lives. He himself had once been all three.

Maher was an incredibly colorful character, possessed of seemingly bottomless energy, great wit, and gigantic ego. One especially notable aspect of his personality was the way he spoke. He did so at amazing speed, offering up fully formed ideas, fully shaped and delivered.

And his talk was laced with more profanity per sentence than I have ever heard in my life. It was simply *blue* with obscenity, but inventively and hilariously so. There was a kind of Mametean poetry to it, only better than that because Maher didn't repeatedly strike a single note, as Mamet's characters sometimes do. He was a full orchestra of profanity.

I interviewed Maher over the course of three or four days, thinking all the while that I was going to come away with a fantastic piece, and one that would pretty much write itself. All I'd have to do was quote him.

But when I got home and began to transcribe my tapes, I quickly realized that Maher's *spoken* sentences—which I had heard in his presence, with the tempering elements of air and kinetic life encircling him—were, when literally transferred to the concentrated page, overwhelmed by all the profanity to a point of incomprehension.

And I realized that in order to re-create in print the exact effect of Maher actually speaking, I would have to weed from his language some of that marvelous profanity. That on the page, less was, not *more* than, but much closer to being the *same* as his spoken language.

Here's the point: If we think of Maher's quotations as dialogue, a certain *stylization* was required in order to make it a close duplicate of his actual speech.

In an essay in his collection *Wormholes*, John Fowles writes: "The most real dialogue is not the most conformable to actual speech. One has only to read a transcribed tape of actual conversation to realize that it is, in a literary context, not very real." Fictional "dialogue is a form of shorthand, an *impression* [italics mine] of what people actually say."

Fowles made these observations as he was writing *The French Lieutenant's Woman*, and, interestingly, he goes on to say that his difficulty, unique to the challenge of writing dialogue for Victorian characters, was, that "genuine dialogue in 1867, (insofar as it can be heard in books of the time) is far too close to our own to sound convincingly old. It . . . fails to agree with our psychological picture of the Victorians—it is not stiff enough, euphemistic enough, and so on—so . . . I have to start cheating and pick out the more formal and archaic (even for 1867) elements of spoken speech."

Already then, in thinking about dialogue, we have these

invaluable terms: shorthand; impression; cheating. To which I would add the word *code*, which I'll say more about later on in the chapter.

If we accept the idea that dialogue is a stylized version of actual speech, why do we employ it? That is, posing the most basic of questions, what does dialogue do, what are its functions, beyond the obvious one of representing spoken speech?

One thing dialogue helps to do is keep the narrative moving. If stasis is the enemy of effective narrative, and it is, then dialogue is one of the weapons we can use in the effort to advance it. Here again it becomes readily apparent why fictional dialogue is a stylized version of actual speech. Because in real conversation, the only two parties the speaker wishes to engage, or inform, or in some way entertain, are the person he is speaking to, and also himself. He and the recipient, or recipients, make up the audience.

But fictional dialogue has a more dimensional obligation than does actual conversation. Unlike real life, in the universe of fiction there is always a third party present, whose unique attendance changes the terms utterly. This third party is, of course, the reader, who is forever "listening." So, again unlike real life, where the flow and power of a conversation pertain only to the speakers, conversation in fiction is principally mindful of a recipient who is positioned outside, beyond the page. And it is this third party, the reader, for whom the conversation is actually intended. To whom the dialogue is responsible. To whom it is obliged. This never-absent figure—the reader/listener—is a concept so fundamental as to seem overly obvious, and yet the nature of a great deal of dialogue by new writers suggests that a reader's presence is something either overlooked, or ignored, or somehow misunderstood.

Maybe we can sense the impact and the demands the reader/listener makes on fictive conversation if we return to the office Christmas party in the previous chapter.

Here, among the revelers in the chandeliered ballroom, is the couple in the corner by the bar that the narrator mentioned, she with her nose ring, he with his tiny dog, a Yorkshire puppy, hidden in a straw basket.

While they are talking to each other, they become aware of someone lingering within earshot and listening intently to every word they say. Furthermore, the eavesdropper is someone they both want to impress. Maybe it's the woman's boss, who is taking some perverse pleasure in standing there, pretending not to notice while being aware that his presence is causing the two of them to perform.

In any case, whoever he is, the effect, I would say the guaranteed effect, of his being there is to raise the energy, the effort, to heighten the consideration that goes into the man and the woman's conversation. This is not to say their conversation will necessarily improve. They may feel so much pressure to perform that they begin to sound like fools. Maybe they are already fools and they only become worse fools. But what is certain, by way of human nature, is that they will consciously try to avoid the inane, the banal, the witless meander. They will hope to sound intelligent, unique, and arresting, in order to hold the interest and earn the good opinion of the eavesdropper.

It is clear where this analogy is going. As fiction writers, we must always remember that there is someone, called a reader, who is eavesdropping, relentlessly, on our characters' conversations; someone whom it is our obligation to impress. Someone who will quite legitimately regard our characters as lackluster and worse if we subject him to the meaningless exchanges that always threaten to become the stuff of dialogue. If, to underline where this began, we do not use dialogue to *advance the narrative* and keep the eavesdropper engaged, he will turn his back on our characters and head off to find some others who will.

This eavesdropping reader is very selfish, very self-involved. And he has good reason and every right to be, because the thing he possesses—his willingness to be interested—awards him enormous respect. He certainly has no obligation to us as writers—nothing beyond that willingness. So it might seem, to an outsider unfamiliar with the terms, that he brings nothing to the table, so to speak. Nothing beyond his curiosity about what our characters are saying to each other. But of course this curiosity is an invaluable offering, an incalculable generosity.

It is not as though the reader/eavesdropper bears an adversarial attitude. He has accepted the invitation, after all. He's been glad to come to the party. It is simply that there are a hell of a lot of conversations going on in the room, the ballroom of literature, and if ours does not hold his attention, then you can be sure, as I said, that he will move along to seek out one that will.

I referred to dialogue as one of the weapons at our disposal in the fight against stagnant narrative. And if used correctly and inventively, it is a highly versatile one. So I want to make sure we recognize just what the mere presence of dialogue signals to the reader. I am not talking now about what the characters are saying to one another, but about the simple decision on a writer's part to use dialogue in the first place. Why, at a certain juncture in a story, would a writer choose to employ it, as opposed to all the other tools of craft available: description, summary, paraphrase, et cetera?

In other words, if a writer conceives of a reader moving

along through a story and decides at some point to have him encounter an exchange of dialogue, the question to be asked is—why dialogue, why here?

For one thing—and running the risk of sounding simplistic—dialogue signals, intentionally or not, that the particular information being presented *as* dialogue is relatively important, is comparably high in the story's hierarchy of impact.

Narrative moves, or should, at a varying pace. It speeds up, it slows down, it speeds up again. It sails along at a fine summarial clip and then it pauses for a stretch to look more closely, in more detail. Without such a pattern of stresses and breaks, the music of narrative is unsurprising, monotonic, and becomes at best a soporific hybrid of Philip Glass and white noise.

When I say narrative speeds up and slows down, I am not talking about the speed at which a reader reads the words. Rather, I am speaking of the patience, if you will, with which the narrative itself inspects its universe—accepting the premise that the more patience which is devoted to that inspection, the more slowly it goes. So it surely follows that when narrative pauses to spend relatively more time looking at its material, it is saying to the reader—how could it not?— *Hey. This is somehow particularly important.*

Annie Dillard, in an essay, "Notes for Young Writers," says it this way: "If something in your narrative is important, give it proportional space. I mean, actual inches [on the page]. The reader has to spend time with a subject to care about it."

Try that as an exercise. Take your story and get out a tape measure to see if those aspects that you have judged to be the more important literally take up proportionally more space— four inches deep on the page versus half an inch, or two pages versus two moderately sized paragraphs. And if you say everything in your story is equally important, you're unclear on the concept.

We can think of this same essential principle in slightly another way, if we pose the question: How *closely* does the narrative ask the reader to stand to the material? And here we bring back the idea of the reader "listening" to the story.

Imagine one more time the office Christmas party. The couple with the dog is still standing near the bar, though the woman's boss, or whoever he was, has gone off to intimidate somebody else.

But now they draw the attention of another guest, who stands unnoticed by herself in the middle of the room. Say, the girlfriend's nose ring reflects the light from the chandelier overhead. And the straw basket reminds the woman watching them of one she herself bought in the mountains of Peru.

Now she sees the girlfriend reaching into the basket and withdrawing the Yorkshire puppy. Her boyfriend shakes his head. He takes the dog and snatches it back. The woman watching all this is naturally curious and therefore moves a bit nearer to get a better view. The closer distance satisfies her briefly, until she sees the couple starting to speak to each other with growing animation. From where she stands, she can't discern their mood. All she knows for sure is that the two of them are speaking, and with increasing feeling.

So what does she do now? Again, I will stop here because I'm sure the point is clear. She moves still closer. She desires to decrease the distance between herself and the moment she is observing. Put purely in terms of a reader and a story, she is drawn closer to this narrative, first, as it offers her details—the nose ring, the straw bag—and interesting action—the tug of war with the dog. And second, as it beckons her even closer, increases her attention, once the characters start to speak.

All this is to say that when you use dialogue, it is as certain as a law of physics that you are inviting your reader to come close to what is happening on the page. And if you do not understand that this is dialogue's effect, if you use dialogue when there is no need to ask readers to come close, then you have called them for no reason. You have asked them instead to listen to speech that has no special impact. Consequently, your dialogue is exposed, because of their sharpened attention, as a flat, tedious drag on your story.

Staying with the notion just a bit longer, think of someone in a public setting—a restaurant, say; a crowded lecture—turning to his partner and saying, "Please, don't make a scene." Or, if the request comes too late, "You're making a scene." We all know what this means. Someone is losing it, or has lost it, is speaking heatedly—maybe shouting—and his companion is asking him to please check it. Why? Because the embarrassed companion anticipates the other customers in the restaurant, the other people at the lecture, turning to watch and listen.

So; two elements. First, a suddenly more elaborate speech and behavior. Second, a sense of heightened attention from the others in the room. These are just the issues that need to be weighed in deciding, in our fiction, if we should "make a scene." Is the moment in the story significant enough to be awarded such full treatment? Does it deserve speech; dialogue? Does it ask for more fully developed behavior, which in fiction making obviously does not have to be anger, can be any emotion—ecstasy, sorrow, even contemplation—in order to summon a reader's closer focus?

You should continuously be asking yourself as you write, *Is now the time, is this the place, for me to "make a scene"?*

The phone rings and the story quotes a character saying,

"Hello?"

And another character saying, "Hello, Anne? Is that you?"

"Yes," says Anne.

"This is Burl," says Burl.

"Oh, hi, Burl."

This is the sort of ordinary, punctuating discourse that has no right or reason to be afforded the distinction of dialogue. But it is just the kind of thing that often does appear in the work of new writers. Maybe this is true, not only because the placement and power of dialogue is not yet understood, but also because it is so easy to "hear" characters speaking in this mundane way. We all do, all the time, without variation. So perhaps new writers reach for it with a sense of relief: They write, *Hello?* and then they write, *Hello*. And think to themselves, I know I got that right.

But the context, as always, is everything: It is now the day after the Christmas party and the woman with the nose ring is visiting her boyfriend after work. She opens the door, takes off her coat, and calls, "Honey, I'm here. Where are you?" And from the kitchen, where he's giving the Yorkshire terrier a bath in the sink, he says, "Oh, hi, hon. I didn't know you were coming."

This is what Annie Dillard, in her essay, calls TV dialogue and it has no business in a story. There is not a reason in the world to ask your reader to come closer, to listen attentively, to such empty give-and-take. There is no possible justification for using up some of the store of dialogue's precious intimacy on such a moment. The woman comes in, takes off her coat, calls to her boyfriend, and then walks into the kitchen to see him washing the dog. Nothing is at stake. Even told in summary, this is all hopelessly inane.

However, I said that context is everything: Once again, the woman with the nose ring opens the door, takes off her coat and calls, "Honey, I'm here. Where are you?" And from the bedroom, where he and his secret lover lie naked in the sheets, he responds, "Oh, hi, hon. I didn't know you were coming."

Exactly the same dialogue is used in the two scenes. But in the latter, I think it is fair to say, there's a lot at stake for the characters. What we have here is a situation. And we want the reader to get near enough to feel its pressure, the delicious discomfort of it. Were you to summarize the scene, without dialogue, you would forfeit the intimacy and readers would not feel nearly so strongly the awful squirming tension of the moment.

If we can agree on the vitality and the effect of strong dialogue, what are some of the characteristics that make it so?

I mentioned earlier the word *code*, and what I have in mind by that is the sense, when reading effective dialogue, that those who are having the conversation are speaking in a kind of private code. It is the sense that the language they use and the references they make tap a common well of knowledge that they alone are privy to.

But wait a minute. Doesn't that contradict the whole premise we have agreed on: that dialogue is actually written for that third party, the reader who is listening in?

Actually, it doesn't, and therein lies the necessary skill. Well-crafted dialogue sounds as though its speakers are conversing exclusively while all the while it's utterly mindful of the reader. It's illusion. It's a delicate balancing act. And it once again relies on the psychology of overheard conversation. For what more reliably beckons and teases the interest of the eavesdropper than listening in on talk he only partially understands? He gets enough to sense the general drift, while working to connect the conversational dots, reach for and grasp the subterranean logic. It is lovely maddening sport, and the writer of dialogue counts on its titillating properties.

There is, then, an essential obliqueness in good dialogue that gives the reader enough—but not too much (and more on that shortly). And often, the dialogue gradually reveals more and more of its subject matter as the conversation unfolds. In which case you as the writer have to decide how much, and when, to divvy out the information that your characters have, and that your reader wants.

As I said we would in the previous chapter, I want again to examine the opening of William Kennedy's novel *Legs*, which provides a fine illustration of dialogue's orchestrated revelation:

1. "I really don't think he's dead," I said to my three very old friends.

2. "You what?" said Packy Delaney, dropsical now, and with only four teeth left . . .

    "He don't mean it," Flossie said, dragging on and then stubbing out another in her chain of smokes . . .

    Tipper Kelley eyed me and knew I was serious.

    "He means it all right," said Tipper, still the dap newsman, but in a 1948 double-breasted. "But of course he's full of what they call the old bully-bull-bullshit because I was there. You *know* I was there, Delaney."

    "Don't I know it," said the Pack.

3. "Me and Bones McDowell," said the Tip. "Bones sat on his chest."

    "We know the rest," said Packy.

    "It's not respectful to Bones' memory to say he sat on the man's chest of his own accord," Tipper said. ". . . Bones wouldn't of done that to any man, drunk or sober, him or Jack the corpse. God rest his soul. Both their souls, if Jack had a soul."

    "He had a soul all right," said Flossie. "I saw that and everything else he had too."

4. "We'll hear about that another time," said Tipper. "I'm now talking about Bones, who with myself was the first up the stairs before the cops . . . The door was open so Bones . . . took a step and tripped, the simple bastard, and sprawled backward over the bed, right on top of poor Jack, in his underwear, who of course didn't feel a thing. Bones got blood all over his pants." . . .

5. "Say what you will," I told them, . . . remembering [the] autopsy myself, remembering Jack's face intact but the back of his head blow away by . . . three soft-nosed .38-caliber bullets . . . I still don't think he's dead."

Passage 1. If we divide this conversation into the five stages indicated, we know after reading, or hearing, the initial declaration that the narrator is in some way suspicious of someone else's death. And that is all we know. We do not yet know who the narrator is, or who it is that is either dead, or not. Neither do we know why the narrator feels there are grounds for suspicion. Finally, we have no idea who the narrator is addressing, or where he is.

Passage 2. Now we know quite a bit more, including the identities of the "three old friends." We have pretty clear evidence that this is an Irish gathering and we learn that the narrator is regarded by at least one of the others as a bullshitter. Because of the tone of the debate, we are beginning to sense that the subject of the conversation is, or was, someone special, since all four are reminiscing so eagerly about him. And we read that one of those gathered, Tipper Kelly, claims to have witnessed the death that the narrator disputes.

But we still do not know who the narrator is, or who may or may not be dead.

Passage 3. During the third stage, we learn of another participant on the night of the disputed death, Bones McDowell, who—which apparently no one disputes—has since died. Too, we get the idea, from the line, "We know the rest," that this conversation has taken place before, which does not inhibit anyone's readiness to be having it again.

Furthermore, we at last have a name for the subject of the discussion, *Jack*, who was (or still is?) someone less than pure ("If Jack had a soul"), and whom Flossie knew intimately.

Passage 4. This passage of descriptive dialogue contains many more details of the night "Jack" died, which makes it increasingly difficult to imagine how the still-unidentified narrator can be clinging to the belief that he didn't.

Passage 5. But cling to it he does. By this point, it is also known that the narrator, in some as yet unrevealed capacity, saw Jack's autopsy. But we still have nothing more than Jack's name. As for the narrator, we do not even have that.

So, as the conversation progresses there is a gradual release of knowledge to readers and the story of *Legs* is quite effectively launched.

If dialogue works best when it achieves a balance between giving the reader too little and too much information, it may be that it functions at its tightest, highest level when it operates at that point of exact tension between obliqueness and obviousness.

If readers have too little, they are of course going to feel confused and become quickly estranged. There is not enough promise held out to them that they are ever going to get what they need to ground themselves. But giving them too much is equally unwise, leaving them potentially overinformed and uninterested. One form of this excess is, simply, repetitiveness, allowing the characters to say the same things over and over. (Which is another way in which dialogue is different from real talk. Actual conversation is amazingly repetitive.) Another version allows each character to go on far too long. (Also a difference from actual conversation.)

And *another* associated manifestation of offering too much is the cardinal sin of smuggling in expository information as dialogue. Never. Ever. Do this. If you want to pass along a block of information necessary to your story, simply give it to readers as straight narrative. Just unapologetically offer it up.

Often, new writers compound the mistake of expository dialogue by composing scenes that feature a character being told something he already knows about himself. This is an impulse, if you think about it, that ironically has the listener, the reader, *too* much in mind, since the information is obviously intended purely for him, rather than for the character, who already knows it.

> "Hi, Fred," said Charisse. "How do you like living in Jacksonville? You've been here almost a year now, since moving from Des Moines."
>
> "Oh, I like it fine," said Fred.
>
> "Good," said Charisse. "I was wondering if you were making new friends, but then you're used to being on your own all these years since your parents died in that terrible car accident when you were only ten."

If you read again the excerpt from *Legs*, you might argue that its dialogue nearly errs in this way. But I think it finally and cleverly manages to avoid the mistake of expository dialogue because the conversation is cast as a commonly remembered barroom tale, a genre that absolutely relies on the recitation of some shared event that each participant offers his dearly held version of. Indeed, the principal *reason* for the conversation is to feel the kind of comradely argument that its very predictability brings.

I once got great advice from a teacher who said, when writing dialogue, to "start at the bottom of the page." What he meant by this, perhaps it needs no explanation, was that we all take a while as writers to get to that place where our fictional conversations indispensably start.

We have our characters talking back and forth, and we are believing all the while that what we have them saying is vital. But a second look reveals that the true meat of their discussion begins further, sometimes quite a bit further along, actually starts, that is, toward the bottom of the page.

This is only a natural progression in the writing process, what I think of as an inevitable sort of throat clearing, before we get to the point. It is the way we all find our way to what we want to say, and it is of course as true for prose as for dialogue. But dialogue's architecture is more exposed, which makes its parts more easily detectable and its flow easier to isolate: She says this line. He responds. And so on, back and forth. And while it is more truly an issue of revision, the idea of starting at the bottom of page is still valuable to keep in mind when you are first composing.

Taking it even further, I have come to recognize at least in my own writing how often the dialogue is improved if I consider "starting with the second sentence." Or the "second phrase." I have noticed how often my characters' conversations move more energetically and with a better carrying cadence if I delete the first sentence of a speech. Or the first phrase, if there are two or three. Or the first word, if there are a few.

So the line:	"Oh, I don't know. Why not?"
Becomes:	"Why not?"
And the exchange:	"Just where is it again?"
	"Where's what?"

Becomes: "Where is it again?"
                         "What?"

Such winnowing is another application of the same throat-clearing principle, reduced now to the microcosm of the line and even to the individual utterance.

Implicit in the need to pare and refine our dialogue is another characteristic that is always present when it is working successfully: energy. The opening of *Legs*, again, is a fine demonstration of fictional conversation moving with a fueling energy. But energy does not always mean brevity. Long uninterrupted speeches can, and must, also convey great energy. They should be composed, just as is the quick, distilled exchange, so that there is nothing wasted, no slackness, so that they are tightly rhythmic.

A monologue from John Cheever's novel *The Wapshot Scandal*, in which an egomaniacal director of a research institute is being questioned before a Senate committee, offers us an extended but highly energetic bit of speech:

> "Dr. Cameron?" One saw this time an old man, slim and with the extraordinary pallor of an uncommonly long life span . . .
>
> "Yes," the doctor said.
>
> "I was born in a small town, Dr. Cameron," the old man said.
>
> "I think the difference between this noisy and public world in which we now live and the world I remember is quite real, quite real . . . I have lived through five wars, all of them bloody, crushing, costly and unjust, and I think inescapable, but in spite of this evidence of man's inability to live peacefully with his kind I do hope that the

world, with all its manifest imperfections, will be preserved . . . I am told that you are famous, that you are esteemed and honored everywhere and I respect your honors unequivocally but at the same time I find in your thinking some narrowness, some unwillingness, I should say, to acknowledge those simple ties that bind us to one another and to the gardens of the earth." . . . [H]is old shoulders shook with a sob. "We possess Promethean powers but don't we lack the awe, the humility, that primitive man brought to the sacred fire? Isn't this a time for uncommon awe, supreme humility? If I should have to make some final statement, and I shall very soon for I am nearing the end of my journey, it would be in the nature of a thanksgiving for stout-hearted friends, lovely women, blue skies, the bread and wine of life. Please don't destroy the earth, Dr. Cameron," he sobbed. "Oh, please, please don't destroy the earth." (170)

Why is this sustained passage so palpably energetic? First of all, I think, it starts at the bottom of the page. The information that begins the speech is quite necessary to establishing the context of the speech. Second, its internal logic does not slacken for a moment. In fact, if you examine it, it is a kind of classically structured rhetorical argument. Thesis. Antithesis. Synthesis: You are brilliant, Dr. Cameron. But your brilliance, alas, has rendered you arrogant and insensitive to the awesome mysteries of life. Therefore, please redirect your brilliance inward so that some sensitivity within you will be stirred and you can use your mind to a less destructive purpose.

The old senator's speech is also wonderfully rhythmic in a way that continuously carries a listener along with it as it crests, and crests, and crests. For example: "I have lived through five wars, all of them *bloody, crushing, costly* and *unjust.*"

And: "You are *famous* . . . you are *great* . . . you are es*teemed* and *honored everywhere*."

Finally, and not incidentally, the old senator's speech is very funny, which always indicates, indeed is inherently a form of, energy.

You should keep in mind that each speaker in a passage of dialogue brings his own quite private agenda to the conversation. All we need to do is look at the word itself to get a sense of what we are talking about here. *Di-alogue*. The representation of crisscrossing logics. So when you write dialogue, you are presenting the individual ideas, opinions, biases—presenting, that is, the logic—of each character as he or she voices it.

In his introduction to the collected novels of Henry Green, John Updike says that "to write how people talk one must know how they think, and an aggressive psychology and sociology [must inform the writer's] articulations on behalf of others."

The word "aggressive" is an interesting one here, and Updike uses it, in the context of his admiration for Green, to contrast the effort actually required to write convincing dialogue with the mistaken notion that it is—Updike's words— "merely a passive gift." (As I read that phrase I assume he has in mind the woeful I-just-listen-to-my-characters-talking-to-me-and-copy-down-what-they-say school of writing.)

"To write how people talk one must know how they think." This would seem elemental, but it is my sense that inexperienced or untalented writers often do not explore their characters deeply enough to be able to answer the question of how they think. What is their private logic? And hence, how do they talk?

When you gather your characters and start them talking, you have the chance to create a great ensemble strength, one of

them feeding off of another, the whole—to use an apt cliché—
being greater than the sum of its parts. But in order for this to
happen, the dialogue must reveal each character's agenda,
using the word as defined by the *Oxford English Dictionary*.
Agenda: "matters of belief; matters of ritual."

Oscar Wilde said, "All dialogue is interruption." And the
inevitable dynamic of constant interruption might be
described as a kind of friction, a lively abrasion, as the various
lines of dialogue move past one another, sometimes missing
altogether, sometimes touching or scraping as they pass, a kind
of sideswiping of requests and questions and assertions, sometimes resulting in a rare full-frontal collision. Dialogue as the
careening paths of bumper cars.

Denis Johnson's story "Emergency" illustrates extremely
well the ways in which characters' self-interests confront
one another. From the many comic examples in this finally
moving story here are five from just the first few scenes. And
as an aside, one of the reasons this story serves so well to
illustrate the point of private agendas is that the two main
characters in the story are on drugs for much of it. Johnson
wonderfully evokes that locked-on, tightly fixated preoccu-
pation of the drugged state: agendas honed to an especially
great degree.

> I'd been working in the emergency room for about three
> weeks, I guess. This was in 1973, before the summer ended.
> With nothing to do on the overnight shift but batch the
> insurance reports . . . I started wandering around, looking
> for Georgie, the orderly, a pretty good friend of mine. He
> often stole pills from the cabinets.

1. He was running over the tiled floor of the operating
   room with a mop. "Are you still doing that?" I said.
   "Jesus, there's a lot of blood here," he complained.

"Where?" The floor looked clean enough to me.

"What the hell were they doing in here?" he asked me.

2. "They were performing surgery, Georgie," I told him.

    "There's so much goop inside us, man," he said, "and it all wants to come out." He leaned his mop against a cabinet.

3. "What are you crying for?" I didn't understand.

    He stood still . . . Then he grabbed the mop and started making broad random arcs with it, trembling and weeping and moving all around the place really fast. "What am I *crying* for?" he said. "Jesus. Wow. Oh, boy. Perfect."

4. I was hanging out in the E.R. with a fat, quivering Nurse. One of the family service doctors that nobody liked came in looking for Georgie to wipe up after him. "Where's Georgie?" this guy asked.

    "Georgie's in O.R.," Nurse said.

    "Again?"

    "No," Nurse said. "Still."

    "Still? Doing what?"

    "Cleaning the floor."

    "Again?"

    "No," said Nurse. "Still."

5. Back in O.R., Georgie dropped his mop and bent over in the posture of a child soiling its diapers. He stared down with his mouth open in terror.

    He said, "What am I going to do about these fucking *shoes*, man?"

    "Whatever you stole," I said, "I guess you already ate it, right?"

    "Listen to how they squish," he said, walking around carefully on his heels.

"Let me check your pockets, man."

He stood still a minute, and I found his stash. I left him about two of each, whatever they were. "Shift is about half over," I told him.

"Good. Because I really, really, really need a drink," he said. "Will you please help me get this blood mopped up?"

Passage 1. Here, it's clear—"Are you still doing that?" "Jesus, there's a lot of blood in here"—that Georgie, his mind seriously chemically altered, and the narrator, sober for the moment, are speaking right past one another.

Passage 2. In this exchange, there is at least a partial influence of one agenda on the other. The narrator explains that surgery has been performed and Georgie, in response, seems to have heard this, in a fashion, while holding tightly to his own impressions: "There's so much goop inside us, man."

Passage 3. Again, there is a partial recognition, resulting in a near-communication: "What are you crying for?" "What am I crying for?" After which, Georgie again subsides into his utterly private world, mumbling to himself: "Jesus. Wow. Oh, boy, perfect."

Passage 4. Here, the conversation between the nurse and the doctor is fully sympathetic, with identical agendas. The two of them are, to begin with, both sober. And they understand all too well their common problem: the predictably wasted Georgie.

Passage 5. Johnson begins this passage with Georgie and the narrator once again speaking with a pure selfishness. Georgie's question, "What am I going to do about these shoes?" is followed by a response that wholly ignores it: "Whatever you stole, I guess you already ate it all, right?" But then, wonderfully, a kind of final couplet of communication occurs: "Shift is about half over." "Good, because I really . . . need a drink."

With the notion of private agendas still in mind, I offer another image. It is of political candidates engaged in one of those dreadful, televised, inaptly named "debates," where they constantly toss back and forth the plea to answer the question. Why won't you just answer the question?

The candidates are determined to make their points, drive home their agendas, and never mind what is actually being asked. But what is irritating in the extreme about the depth of drivel to which so-called political debate has fallen is, happily, one of the marks of successful dialogue—a pattern of give and take in which the characters do not answer the questions, or answer them only partially, or appropriate them to satisfy their private agendas.

Two things above all. First, view the writing of dialogue with the importance it absolutely requires, and not as an opportunity to relax and coast a bit after struggling with the demands of sentences. Maybe one of the chief reasons so many new writers—assuming they have talent—write such dreadful dialogue is because they believe it is comparatively easy. They think, "Making a character *talk?* Hell, I can do that. I talk. Everybody talks." But this kind of thinking, to whatever extent it occurs, mistakenly assumes the writing of dialogue to be, as Updike says, "a mere passive gift."

It is not. It requires "an aggressive psychology and sociology [informing] articulations on behalf of others." Those others, of course, are your characters.

Second, *listen.* And steal. Steal blatantly. Become yourself, in life, that eavesdropper I was earlier imagining. As Eudora Welty says, "Think of your ears as magnets."

I was standing one day outside a garage, waiting for the mechanic to finish working on my car, and there were two other men, who knew each other, standing nearby talking.

The subject of their conversation was a woman they both knew, and they were speaking in a very admiring, if hugely politically incorrect, way about her. The conversation went something like:

> "Yeah. She is fine."
> "She sure is."
> "And you know, she ain't dumb either."
> "As a matter of fact, she ain't a *bit* dumb."
> "You know, I like that," said the first man. "I like a chick with 'two and two makes four.'"

I like a chick with "two and two makes four." Well, that seemed like a pretty great line to me. So I stole it, and gave it to a character in *Dexterity*, my first novel, where the conversation became:

> They all sat in silence, then complained for quite a while about the heat. They talked of the new girl from Mellenville working at Dee's Luncheonette, whose [body] strained impressively her lime-green uniform, and who also seemed capable of keeping food orders straight.
> "She's got a real quick mind," Ewel Chesley said seriously.
> "I like a chick with two and two makes four," said Tommy Beener.

Considering the subject of dialogue, I naturally looked at some writers—for the first time, in some cases; rereading them in others—whose work readily comes to mind when a new writer asks, "Who should I read as a model of great dialogue?" And what I found was that a lot of that work from the fairly recent past seemed dated.

I wonder if being recognized as exemplary, at a given cultural moment, sometimes means that the dialogue relies on a savvy timeliness, which is, therefore, more vulnerable to time, more likely perishable? Perhaps such a writer's ear catches but then too fully depends on the tics and mannerisms of a certain period, or a particular social stratum. And if so, does that overdependency almost guarantee a datedness?

Ironically, maybe the same lesson I discussed at the outset applies here: the mistaken assumption that an exact transcript of conversation is ideal dialogue. I certainly do not mean that if a writer has a great ear, he or she should plug it. But if a writer places too much faith in the current vernacular, it is, in a way, as if he or she were giving us a too literal transcript. So what seems, when we read it, all aglitter with style is, in fact, actually not stylized enough—as we have taken the word to mean "a shaped impression."

If so, where does that leave us on the subject of successful dialogue? Maybe here: that the larger challenge is, as Updike says, to go deeply into your characters in an effort to know how they think and respond. And to write dialogue, as a result, that does not too fully depend on the faddish phrase, on the pace and cadence of the moment. A moment that is sure to pass.

4

Characters

The Need for Flawed Heroes and Sympathetic Villains

In E. M. Forster's classic book *Aspects of the Novel*, he devotes two chapters to a discussion of fictional characters where, among other things, he offers his useful distinction between those who are flat and those who are round. And he begins by observing that "the actors in a story are, or pretend to be, human beings. Since the [fiction writer] is also a human being, there is an affinity between him and his subject matter which is absent in many other forms of art." This logic would only follow from the fact that he titled these chapters on characters "People," and I love what he said, in part because it is typical of the combination of wit and homely wisdom throughout the book. And also because the two ideas—characters as human beings, and the writer's affinity with his characters—are at the base of what must influence the drawing of them in realistic fiction.

I want to get at the issue by offering up the proposition that all fictional characters must be complex. And they must be sympathetic, which requires Forster's "affinity" between the writer and his subject matter. And following that, I would say that the way to this necessary complexity is *through* sympathy. The task, then, for the writer is to present villainous, ignoble, antiheroic characters sympathetically. And to depict admirable, noble, heroic characters as flawed. Self-evident as this sounds, one of the major problems in the fictional creations of beginning writers is an absence of complexity. Instead of meeting characters drawn with some measure of inner contradiction, the stories are populated by heroes of unblemished, blinding goodness and villains of unrelieved evil.

The terms *heroes* and *villains* connote I suppose the grand gestures of sentimental melodrama. Simon Legree tying the heroine to the railroad track. But I think that's all right, as a place to start, when you begin to conceive a character. There is nothing wrong with thinking of the primary characters in a work of fiction as heroic or villainous. In fact, it seems to me that the subtle psychological and emotional movement of serious fiction essentially has to do with charting the ebb and flow of the contest between the hero and the villain.

But this blueprint becomes insufficient when writers create such extremes of virtue and villainy as to make their characters—and, inevitably, the situations they inhabit—implausible, and therefore dismissible, and therefore incapable of holding a reader's interest. A single-shaded character is an uncompleted character and an uncompleted character is an uninteresting one.

The key in all this, as I said, is sympathy. But let's be clear just what that means. First of all, it does not mean that every character should be likable. I cannot imagine a more certain road to unreadability than working toward the goal of creating a whole population of "likable" characters. I cannot even imagine a writer asking himself the question—am I making Bill or Charlotte or Aunt June likable? For one thing, it would presuppose the guaranteed result of mixing the various qualities that go into forming a particular character, measuring them and balancing them in the right proportion, following some recipe for a final likability. But of course that's not how it works. Writers, contemplating their characters, try to figure out what motivates them. How they think. How they will react. What emotions they will display in a variety of situations. They do not think: "If I give her a large amount of will-fulness, about half that much vulnerability, and just a touch of vanity, she'll be, *voila*, likable."

I have, in fact, often heard writers say, "I like all my characters." Well, maybe so. But I hope that does not mean they are all likable or that their creators regard them as such. I would rather believe that these writers have in mind the vital symbiosis of sympathy with their characters. By which I mean, as the *Oxford English Dictionary* defines sympathy: "The fact or capacity of entering into or sharing the feelings of another."

In other words—"I feel your pain." Absurd as that phrase has become, with all the baggage attached to it, that is just what writers should say—or be able to say—to their characters. Your pain, and your pleasure, and whatever else in between. Because unless writers feel it in making a character, what chance does a reader have to feel it when asked to receive that character?

John Gardner, in *The Art of Fiction*, uses the term *frigidity* to get close to this same notion, although he extends the discussion beyond characters to the whole of the writer's material. Frigidity, Gardner says, "occurs in fiction whenever the author . . . is less concerned with his characters than he ought to be—less concerned, that is, than any decent human being observing the situation would naturally be." Here again there is a resonance of Forster: writers are human beings; their characters are human beings; given this coincidence, an affinity should result.

Gardner goes on to identify frigidity as the culprit responsible for all kinds of crimes in fiction writing: sentimentality; mannered prose; the bloodless tinkering with form at the expense of heartfelt story. I happen to agree with his catalog of the crimes, whether or not there is a single perpetrator. And I don't mean to split hairs when I say that Gardner's extremely valuable idea of frigidity, and mine of sympathy, certainly overlap even if they don't exactly equate.

Gardner is speaking most of all, as he says, about a writer's absence of *concern* for his characters—and therefore, it would follow, a lack of sympathy. He is talking about a writer not taking characters—or the work of writing generally—seriously enough. But when I speak of an absent sympathy, I am not perforce suspecting a lack of concern or seriousness, but rather a sense that the writer does not know, first of all, that sympathy is required, and, second, how to go about achieving it.

To say that in an ideal fictional world all the characters should be complex suggests even the marginal, supporting players. This might seem to be a goal in opposition to what Forster had in mind when he claimed that characters were either flat or round. Flat ones being, in his words, "constructed round a single idea or quality: when there is more than one factor in them, we get the beginning of the curve towards round."

It is an invaluable distinction. But does a flat character—"constructed round one idea"—necessarily have to be a simplistic one? Why can't a flat character's single idea also have some share of complexity to it? (And I don't mean to suggest that Forster says it can't. He's focusing on issues somewhat different from sympathy and complexity.) Think, for instance, of Dickens's Mrs. Micawber, who, Forster says, "can be expressed in one sentence such as, 'I will never desert Mr. Micawber.' There is Mrs. Micawber—she says she won't desert Mr. Micawber, she doesn't, and there she is."

Fair enough. But I would suggest that in Mrs. Micawber's one-notedness, there is some measure of complexity. On the one hand, she is admirably loyal, boldly dogged. On the other, she is simple-minded, and blind in her attachment. There is a mixture of characteristics in the flatness of Mrs. Micawber. To be blindly loyal is to be both admirably reliable—a redeeming feature—and unfortunately closed-minded—a less appealing one. So to conceive of characters as flat does not prohibit a writer from making them complicated.

Thinking first about the notion of flawed heroes, I am reminded of Orwell's wonderful essay "Reflections on Gandhi." In discussing Gandhi's life, Orwell plays with the conceptions of sainthood and humanness, and if we think of the purely good fictional character as one who is virtually saintly, Orwell's distinctions are extremely helpful. He says, for instance, that while many systems of belief are in some sense founded on the idea that the purer the life—the more successfully one eludes temptation—the higher is the place in the hierarchy such a life deserves to occupy. And furthermore, the thinking goes, the ordinary man fails in this effort because the requirements of the saintly life are simply too difficult. The average man, then, is a failed saint.

But, Orwell says, as a matter of fact, "the essence of being *human* is that one does not seek perfection, that one is sometimes [more than] willing to commit sins for the sake of loyalty . . . and that one is prepared in the end to be defeated and broken up by life, which is the inevitable price of fastening one's love upon other human individuals." He goes on to say, "No doubt alcohol, tobacco, and so forth, are things that a saint must avoid, but sainthood is also a thing that human beings must avoid. . . [Most] people genuinely do not wish to be saints, and it is probable that [those] who . . . aspire to sainthood, have never felt much temptation to be human beings" (176) (italics mine).

I'm sure the point is plain. As Orwell says, the saint—the figure of pure goodness—and the human being are in a real

sense opposites. Opposites in aspiration. And, just as importantly for a fiction writer, opposites in their life experiences.

By which I mean that impossibly good characters are failures not only because they are not credible to a reader. They
are also failures in the help they refuse to provide their creator,
because they don't do the essential job of leading a reader to all
the ambiguities and hypocrisies and other impure episodes that
make up the stuff of life, that make up the stuff of realistic
fiction.

Continuing to look at it from the writer's standpoint:
because purely good characters would by definition stay clear
of ambiguity, hypocrisy, betrayal, and so forth, they provide
their creators with extremely thin material. So for both the
writer, who makes them, and the reader, who is asked to follow
them, these saintly characters would be narrative tour guides
with little stomach for travel, if the episodic road were the
least bit strenuous or unpredictable.

It is true that great writers have written ridiculously good
characters. Dickens's angelic heroines come to mind right
away: Esther Summerson in *Bleak House*, Little Dorrit, as two
good examples. But the fact that such characters emerged from
the mind of a genius does not excuse them. Or give us permission to create some who are like them. They're still groaners,
and we should still regard them as such. What allows them to
survive, in Dickens's case at least, is the tremendously lively
universe they are a part of. In other words, they do not stand in
isolation, where their annoying purity would be more quickly
exposed. They are surrounded by, they function within, a
teeming world filled with wildly foible characters who offset
the deadening virtue of the Esther Summersons and generate
so much energy that they enliven them to some degree.

Perhaps the argument could be made that when confronting narrative whirlwinds as raucous as Dickens's, then a
reader needs a still presence at the center of it all; that is, a

character to function as the eye of the storm. Maybe so, although it is not an argument I would necessarily sign on to. We might need a still presence, but a character can be still without being saccharine.

So, if writers fail to create complex characters in part because they do not know how to sympathize with them, it would be good to look at some helpful technical advice. Some of the best is contained in Wayne C. Booth's *The Rhetoric of Fiction*. It is both difficult, and unfair to Booth, to try to reduce his thoughts and comments on this matter. But I will try to do it anyway, by saying that writers can create sympathy for their characters—sympathy the writer feels, and sympathy the character arouses in the reader—in a couple of ways.

They may, first, through a reliable, omniscient narrator, make an effort to explain the character's behavior. Booth calls this, plainly enough, offering an "apology." And he uses passages from *The Brothers Karamazov* and Graham Greene's *This Gun for Hire* as examples, showing that a narrator whom the reader has come to trust, one who is looking along with the reader at the character's actions, can establish some context—whether it is the character's background, his social environment, his misfiring psyche, some singular haunting circumstance, whatever—that helps to explain his actions. To be clear, the narrative does not for a minute excuse these actions and it certainly does not advocate them. But it does make an effort to help the reader understand them.

A second way of creating sympathy, according to Booth, is to eliminate entirely this intervening objective commentator and instead get thoroughly inside the character's mind. This is of course one of the exhilarating liberties of writing fiction: the invitation, the constant opportunity, to know what your character is thinking and feeling.

Following this strategy of intimacy, a writer can write, a

reader can read, sympathetically because, as Booth puts it—and remember he is speaking of villainous characters—"we know [the character] in a view which in real life we never obtain of anyone but ourselves." In other words, it is possible for a person to know what he himself is thinking and feeling. And it is possible to know what a character is thinking and feeling. But it is impossible to ever fully know, in real life, what someone else is thinking and feeling.

So in writing and reading realistic fiction, when, as Booth says, we can see "the whole [world] through the isolated sufferer's vision, we are forced to feel it through his heart. And it is our sense of his isolation . . . that contributes most to this sympathy."

Elsewhere, Booth writes, "Such isolation can be used to create an almost unbearably poignant sense of the [character's] helplessness in a chaotic, friendless world." So that sometimes, in some stories, "the isolated [character] can do for herself what no other narrator could possibly do for her [or him]."

Do what?

Well, simply put, make the most convincing case for herself to the reader. If writers do not understand—do not sympathize with—their villains, not only are they not able to bring them credibly to the page, they are therefore also unable to make their case—or allow *them* to make their case—to the reader. And in the legal system that is serious literature, every character, good or evil, has the right to make his best case to the reader.

Both of these ways of creating sympathy—employing an omniscient narrator to explain, and fully occupying the character's interior—are, obviously, strategies of narration. But manipulating narrative is by no means the only way to establish sympathy. It can also be developed by qualities in the story or novel's supporting cast that surrounds and competes against the villainous character. That is to say, all things being relative, we inevitably weigh, as readers, one character against another. And if a villain is rebuked, or bullied, or somehow made to suffer at the hand of someone who is nearly as corrupt, then the villain's evil will almost certainly be diffused, if not diluted.

Also, much has to do with the nature, the style, the tone and polish of the character's villainy. Is he or she a glib or stuttering or self-mocking villain? A cold-blooded or an unthinkingly desperate one? Smoothly competent or brutally hapless?

All these factors and others can be illustrated by paying some attention to the personality and performance of Shakespeare's Richard the Third. In a discussion of villainous characters, how could one possibly leave out one of the most inspired villains in all of English literature?

Here is someone who, before we even glimpse him in the play that bears his name, has murdered King Henry the Sixth, who'd reigned most recently, and has helped to murder Henry's son. And who, when we meet him, is setting one of his brothers—King Edward the Fourth—to suspect their third brother, Clarence, of plotting against him, which results in Edward's ordering Clarence killed.

Immediately after which, Richard learns that his brother the king, Edward, is very sick and dying. Hearing this wonderful news, Richard hits on the idea of marrying Lady Anne, which would unite the warring royal families and advance his status as he schemes to be king. There's only one hitch: Lady Anne is the widow of the prince and the daughter-in-law of Henry the Sixth—the two men Richard killed earlier.

But this obstacle only makes for greater sport, so far as Richard is concerned. When he finds Anne, who's escorting the corpse of Henry the Sixth, she says in greeting him that she hopes, if he ever has a son, the child will be so ugly he'll terrify his mother to death. Anne goes on to say that the only way Richard can redeem himself is to hang himself, and points out that Richard is so diabolical his mere presence is causing Henry the Sixth's wounds to open and begin bleeding all over again. Now *that* is evil.

Richard calmly waits her out, then says that actually it was his brother who killed her husband. It is true that all three brothers did have a hand in the murder and Richard's sword was in fact the second to stab Anne's husband. So technically Richard has a point. He has a kind of Clintonesque "While legally accurate" defense going here. And as for Henry the Sixth, Richard says, he really did Henry a favor because he was much better fit for Heaven than for kingship. Which again, is in some sense true. Henry was a terrible king and a most worshipful man.

Then Richard suggests that it's truly *Anne's* fault they're both dead. That he killed them because all he could think about was having her. What's more, to prove how much he worships her, he will kill himself if she orders him to. But she should remember, if she does, then she will be guilty of *three* deaths.

Anne has begun to weaken at this point, and amazingly, by the end of the scene, she has agreed to marry Richard. In response, he says that's great and now he must hurry off to the monastery to see his good friends, the monks.

And so it goes. Quickly afterward, Richard has several more people killed, including the new wife, Anne, and two young princes who are his nephews. Then he suggests to the dead princes' mother that he marry their sister, who is hardly more than a child. Within all this he has people scurrying all over England, doing his bidding, spreading rumors for him—*You do know, don't you, that young Edward's a bastard*—while he spends more time in the monastery, prompting his momentary ally, the Duke of Buckingham, to make sure people are noticing, urging them to look at Richard over there, that "Christian prince," in the company of bishops.

Finally, of course, Richard manipulates folks to plead with him to take the crown.

And then, as we know, once he's got it, things immediately start to unravel. His enemies, led by Richmond, mass against him. Buckingham and others wisely defect before they get their heads lopped off. And in the end, Richmond kills Richard on the battlefield, gets the girl—the young niece Richard planned to marry as soon as the war was over—and becomes king Henry the Seventh.

Now. How can such a heinous creature possibly lay any claim to our sympathy? Well, first remember the definition. Audiences are offered the chance to understand, not *like* Richard. And if we hold to this distinction, I would say that Richard is a sympathetic villain for several reasons. First, he's seen as physically repellent—lame, hunchbacked—and painfully aware of it. Indeed, as he tells us in his first soliloquy, he's so universally mocked "That dogs bark at me as I halt by them." And in those days, when the royal class was thought nearly divine, it is one thing for a commoner to be physically misshapen, quite another for a royal—and a royal male at that—to be so.

Along with this, we see immediately how unanimous is the hatred for Richard, especially among women (who are, interestingly, the far bolder of the sexes in their confrontations with Richard). No sooner does he come face to face with someone than the insults start to fly: "minister of hell"; "defused infection of a man"; "abortive, rooted hog"; "hell's black intelligencer."

Even his mother despises him. The first time we see her she allows as how, "he is my son, and therein my shame," while quickly adding that she is in no way responsible for the way he turned out: "yet from my dugs he drew not his deceit." And the last time they speak, she thinks ruefully how "she might have intercepted thee / By strangling thee in her accursed womb." And ends this thought by calling him "toad, thou toad." His *mother*.

The sheer relentless volume of this invective has a cumulative effect. At least a part of us doesn't like to see anyone ganged up on. Also, some of those who hurl the vitriol are themselves odious, especially old Queen Margaret, whom everyone hates, and his mother, the duchess of York, intent on saving face above all. Which, as I said, serves to make Richard, in their company, seem comparably not quite so spectacularly hateful.

In consequence of all this, I believe, in Booth's words, that we feel to some extent a Richard who is isolated "in a chaotic, friendless world." Certainly the chaos, the friendlessness, and hence the isolation, are entirely his own doing. But there they are, nevertheless, and we're extremely aware of them.

We're especially aware of them because, again from Booth, "we see the whole world through [Richard's] vision" and, therefore, "feel it through his heart." To the degree that Richard has a heart.

And the reason we see the world through Richard's vision is because he turns to us, again and again throughout the play, in soliloquies and punctuating asides, to tell us, and only us, what is really going on; what he is really thinking; what he really has in mind. In other words, we, the audience, and let's say also, for our purposes here, "the readers," are the only ones in his entire world who are taken into his confidence. Everyone else gets at best a partial, scheming version. To them, he behaves duplicitously. But then, after finishing his lying and manipulating, he turns to us, takes off his mask, and tells us the truth. So we are continually invited into his mind, and the unconscious effect of that, I think, is, first, to make us feel strangely grateful and privileged. And second, it allows

Richard to "do for himself what no other narrator could possibly do for him."

I believe we feel sympathy for Richard, too, because there is something about his very hubris, the "bravado and exhilaration" of his "antic cunning" in Herschel Baker's words, that makes us shake our heads with admiration, however reluctantly. When he is at the top of his game, through acts 3 and the first half of 4, we can't help but think, "Damn, this guy is *good!*"

Along with that, we get the sense that he's enjoying himself tremendously, because *he* can't quite believe how good he is. When, for instance, he woos Lady Anne, he gives her his ring, saying, "Look how my ring encompasseth thy finger / Even so thy breast encloseth my poor heart: / Wear both of them, for both of them are thine." Then, after she's left, Richard himself says—again, confidentially to us—"I, that killed her husband and his father . . . And I no friends to back my suit . . . And yet to win her! . . . Hah!"

I will cite, among others, two more reasons why one can regard Richard sympathetically. Near his end, when he's revealed to be a pitiably incompetent leader—a temperament fit for revolt, but not for rule—we see that he's going to lose it all to the good and handsome Richmond. And the underdog impulse inevitably kicks in. We watch as he proves to be a bumbler as a warrior: he sleeps in on the day of the big battle; his pep talk to his army is a narrow, mean-spirited oration, silent any of the higher noble chords Richmond has struck in his. He can't even find his horse. And we gradually come to think, at least a little, in seeing all this, "The poor sap."

And finally, he shows himself to be notably free of whining and self-pity, saying, "If I should die, no one will pity me. And wherefore should they? For I myself find in myself no pity to myself." How many of us could summon such self-candor?

So we leave Richard, we're glad he's done, we're appalled

by the carnage and the homicide. But nevertheless, or so it seems to me, Shakespeare has created a sympathetic villain.

Turning from Shakespeare's England to Toni Morrison's rural Ohio, one might experience a fairly violent head-snap in the radical shift of time and cultures.

I began by saying it should be a writer's ultimate goal to create complex fiction through sympathetic characters. And it seems to me that with *Sula*, the entire novel, from its broadest to its finest strokes, is founded on contradiction and complexity.

Considering just some of the larger examples, Sula's grandmother, Eva, learns that what she would come to feel for her ex-husband was hatred, and it was "hatred that kept her alive and happy." Later, Eva kills her son, burns him up, because he loved her so much he was trying to get back into her womb. Later still, we read that Eva cursed a man every day for thirty-seven years. Why? Because he saved her life. Further on, a young man named Jude marries Sula's best friend, Nel, and his reason for marrying her is to redirect his hatred. Shortly after, when Sula sexually steals Jude from Nel, she sees it as a way of complimenting Nel. She also sees Nel's shattered response as a betrayal of her, Sula—for behaving in the way that other women would, and not as their history of friendship had led Sula to believe Nel would react.

There are more examples: What Nel feels most palpably, after Jude leaves, is the presence of his absence. And her ensuing grief comes to be for the day she will lose her horrible loneliness. Meanwhile, we see how Sula's presence—she is perceived by the town to be the evil witch—is producing wholesale acts of goodness and charity among the townspeople. And conversely, how Ajax, Sula's lover, is good to women. But that his goodness inspires meanness in those he is

kind to. Which leaves Sula, in the aftermath of Ajax's departure, to go to bed with men in order to feel misery and deep
sorrow, because they were what she was able to feel, and she
wanted to feel.

Over and over, then, through the book, we encounter these
deeply imbedded contradictions: loving to feel hatred; killing
out of love; evil inspiring charity; kindness causing evil.

Living in such a richly contradictory atmosphere, the characters who reflect it necessarily emerge bearing the same para-
doxical makeups. Given that inevitability, it is helpful to look
at the ways Morrison works to allow a reader to respond with
sympathy, following the two narrative strategies mentioned
earlier: first, the use of an outside apologist; second, a voice
residing deeply inside the character, free of any intervening
consciousness.

The Outside Apologist

Following the first brief chapter whose opening sentences we
studied earlier, Morrison devotes an entire section, entitled
"1920," told by an omniscient narrator, to explain Nel's
makeup—her almost reflexive "goodness," her timidity, her
suppressed yearning. We read that Helene's mother, Nel's
grandmother, was a Creole whore, from whom Helene fled,
physically and psychologically, as far as she could flee. Over
time, Helene has become a repressively fastidious mother who
shapes Nel into an orderly and obedient young girl.

Paralleling this chapter, the next section, "1921," continues the same omniscient narrative and is given over to Sula's
family's history. The nourishing chaos of grandmother Eva's
house is described. We are told of the bizarre tenants; of the
three Deweys, who are sort of foster children by default; of the
casual sexual commerce enjoyed by Sula's mother, Hannah,

and so on. Raised in this atmosphere, the narrative explains, Sula began to grow—how could she not?—into the compelling moral anarchist she becomes.

There are several more examples of this disinterested narrative sprinkled through the novel, the most significant being a long passage that comes soon after Sula has seduced Nel's husband. It runs to several pages, perhaps an acknowledgment that such an apparently heartless act requires a lengthy and thorough defense.

And a stunning defense it is, arguing on Sula's behalf that she was "[a]s willing to feel pain as give pain." That hers was "an experimental life," the result of a childhood during which she had come to feel that "there was no other that [she] could count on" and "no self to count on either." Sula, we read, "had no center, no speck around which to grow." She also had "no ego." And, "For that reason she felt no compulsion to verify herself—to be consistent with herself" (118–19). And so on, in Morrison's ineffably striking language, for some pages more, all of it summoned, again omnisciently, so that we might be able to *enter into or share the feelings of another*.

The Character's Own Consciousness

As full of art and instruction as these omniscient passages are, there are as many, in *Sula*, that speak directly to the reader from inside the character's thoughts and feelings. In the interest of space, I will offer two, arguably the most powerful examples in the novel.

Both occur as Sula is dying, the first just after Nel comes to visit her and has gone to the drugstore for pain medicine:

> As soon as the door was shut, Sula breathed through her mouth. While Nel was in the room the pain had increased. Now that this new pain killer . . . was on the way her mis-

ery was manageable. She let a piece of her mind lay on Nel. It was funny, sending Nel off to that drugstore right away like that, after she had not seen her to speak to for years . . . . She wondered for an instant what Nellie wanted; why she had come. Did she want to gloat? Make up? Following this line of thought required more concentration than she could muster. Pain was greedy; it demanded all of her attention. But it was good that this new medicine . . . would be brought to her by her old friend. Nel, she remembered, always thrived on a crisis. Nel was the best. When Sula imitated her, or tried to, those long years ago, it always ended up in some action noteworthy not for its coolness but mostly for its being bizarre. The one time she tried to protect Nel, she had cut off her own finger tip and earned not Nel's gratitude but her disgust. From then on she had let her emotions dictate her behavior.

After this, Nel returns with the medicine, and the two achieve at least a partial reconciliation. And when she leaves, we are once again in Sula's mind:

> When Nel closed the door, Sula reached for more medicine. Then she turned the pillow over to its cool side and thought about her old friend. "So she will walk on down that road, her back so straight in that old green coat, the strap of her handbag pushed back all the way to the elbow, thinking how much I have cost her and never remember the days when we were two throats and one eye and we had no price." . . .
>
> Pain took hold. First a fluttering as of doves in her stomach, then a kind of burning, followed by a spread of thin wires to other parts of her body. . . .
>
> So she lay there wondering how soon she would gather enough strength to lift her arm and push the rough quilt

away from her chin and whether she would turn her cheek to the cooler side of the pillow now or wait till her face was thoroughly soaked and the move would be more refreshing. But she was reluctant to move her face for another reason. If she turned her head, she would not be able to see the boarded-up window Eva jumped out of. And looking at those four wooden planks with the steel rod slanting across them was the only peace she had. The sealed window soothed her with its sturdy termination, its unassailable finality. It was as though for the first time she was completely alone—where she had always wanted to be—free of the possibility of distraction. . . .

While in this state of weary anticipation, she noticed that she was not breathing, that her heart had stopped completely. A crease of fear touched her breast, for any second there was sure to be a violent explosion in her brain, a gasping for breath. Then she realized, or rather she sensed, that there was not going to be any pain. She was not breathing because she didn't have to. Her body did not need oxygen. She was dead.

Sula felt her face smiling. "Well, I'll be damned," she thought, "it didn't even hurt. Wait'll I tell Nel."

Not only have we inhabited Sula's mind, she has allowed us to accompany her even as she leaves mortal life, and to stay with her in some immediate hovering afterness.

In making sympathetic characters, it is important to be clear that the goal is not to make a "good" character obversely "bad" or a "bad" character obversely "good." Rather, as *Sula* shows, it is to make both types of characters—all characters—contradictorily complicated. So as writers work to make their heroes flawed and their villains sympathetic, they should keep in mind, most of all, the simple matter of who their characters are, as individuals. If they do that, they will have a better chance at keeping the contradictions they give them within the persuasive context of their personalities.

That is to say, when a writer shows a villain's act of unselfishness or modesty or charity, it will not be on the same order as a hero's generosity. It will still begin in and be generated by the heart of this character who is, in the main, unfavorable. To illustrate, consider a character in another Morrison novel, *The Bluest Eye*.

Cholly Breedlove, the father of a girl named Pecola, comes home drunk one afternoon and finds his young daughter alone in the house. Seeing a gesture she makes that reminds him of the day he met her mother, he is overwhelmed and a kind of generous lust fills him. And what does he do? He rapes her, rapes his daughter. And Morrison—in making the case for Cholly—places this act within an acutely personal climate of language and emotion, speaking of him wanting to give to Pecola the best that was in him.

Morrison writes, "He was the one who loved her enough to touch her, envelop her, give something of himself to her." Convincingly, then, I would argue, she presents Cholly's act as one of love, however unspeakable, one that's perversely generous within the terms of the culture and the character. Cholly's "kindly" action is hardly an impulse of virtuous charity. Rather, it is one of deeply complicated evil.

This is an extreme example, but it makes the point—that writers must give their characters contradictory complexities according to the sense of who they essentially and individually are. A writer cannot have a hero show he is flawed by having him abruptly decide that he should kill his brother. That's an impulse better left to Richard the Third. Neither can a character on the order of Cholly Breedlove be made to show his generous side by going down to the Red Cross to give blood. Contradictions of such polarity aren't complex, they're laughably implausible.

As Morrison says elsewhere in *The Bluest Eye*, "Love is never any better than the lover. Wicked people love wickedly, violent people love violently, weak people love weakly, stupid people love stupidly."

What's vital here for the fiction writer to remember is that the wicked, and the violent and the stupid *do* also love, in their way. Just as humble and loving and thoughtful people also hate. Hate humbly, hate lovingly, hate thoughtfully, and so on.

So a writer should always try to keep in mind how special, and vulnerable, how trusting, fictional people are compared to real ones. As we have seen, it is inherent in their makeup that they invite us in to know them completely. Unlike even those closest to us in real life—our spouses, our lovers, our kin, whom we can never know completely—fictional people retain only as much privacy and secrecy as those of us who create them decide to let them keep. If we want to invade them entirely, it's perfectly all right with them.

That is an offer we never get in real life. Of course, it's an offer we'd never *want* to get in real life. To know someone completely? Thanks, anyway. But in this regard, fiction is something else, as Forster reminds us. "Perfect knowledge is an illusion," he says. "But in [fiction] we can know people perfectly, and apart from the general pleasure of reading, we can find [in writing and reading about fictional people] a compensation for [people's] dimness in life."

How could we possibly view such partners, so willing and so cooperative in the enterprise, with anything other than sympathy?

5

High Events

The Treatment of Dramatic Moments in Serious Fiction

Years ago, one of the best students I have ever worked with gave me a draft of a novel he wanted to revise in our fiction writing workshop through the term. I had not seen any of this work. He'd been admitted to the class on the strength of a long story that showed he had a sophisticated fictional imagination. But besides that, the story he submitted also made it clear that he had a gift for language. And it hinted that he was critically shrewd.

Consequently, I couldn't believe the draft of his novel, which began with the violent death of the male narrator's sister. And which, before one hundred manuscript pages were done, included that sister's twin now being stalked by the dead girl's old boyfriend, who instantly transferred his obsession from one twin to the next; the booze-induced mutual abuse of the narrator's alcoholic parents; and the revelation that the narrator's sexy distant cousin was actually another sister, which meant that they'd been conducting an incestuous relationship.

This manuscript stands out so clearly in my memory because I had never before, and I haven't since, come across a case where a student's mind was so good, the talent so apparent, the purpose so serious, and the fiction so miscast and absurdly conceived. I had never confronted a situation where the two elements—the young writer's potential and admirable ambition on one hand; the misguided writing that resulted on the other—disagreed so dramatically.

When we talked, he explained that he had given his story a multitude of soap-operatic events because he assumed it was the way one attracts and holds and increases a reader's attention. To his credit, he was instinctively uneasy with what he'd done, but had written out of an understanding that such a relentless piling up of plot twists and collisions was necessary.

In a *way*, he was right. Presented with a madcap narrative on the order of this student's, readers might indeed stay with it in a fashion, as they wonder to themselves, "What happens next?" Intelligent readers, however, would fairly quickly come to ask the question with a mixture of amusement and incredulity, as their interest—that prize the writer works to gain and hold—becomes a skimming, shallow one. Why? Because the effect of one extreme episode after another is briefly to divert the reader's mind to each new thing that comes along, while making it impossible—since there's not enough time between these feverishly pitched moments and no single one is developed with any complexity—to deepen and detail and further elaborate his interest.

Until, increasingly numbed to real response, the smart reader's curiosity becomes aimed—not toward the characters and their dilemmas—but away from and out of the story altogether, focusing on the maker of the wildly unlikely concoction. The fundamental question, "What happens next?" then becomes, "What in God's name will he or she, the writer, come *up* with next?"

So, this not uncommon paradox: a new writer, with serious aspiration, includes an excess of events in order to draw readers further in. And unwittingly he creates the opposite effect of denying them even the possibility of journeying more deeply into the story. Instead, they are kept, at best and only briefly, on the story's wildly shifting surface. Because there *is* no depth to such a narrative; there is *only* shifting surface.

The student's story, in other words, was swollen with what I will call "high events," by which I mean, in simplest terms, moments of strong dramatic impact in a story. I use the designation *high* because I tend to visualize the steady, even movement of narrative proceeding along a horizon line. (These qualities of steadiness and evenness are vital, of course, as the narrative progresses, producing the hum of story that lures and holds the reader. The beat of lullaby.) Working the image further, if we imagine for a minute this movement of narrative as the regular pulsing line on a heart monitor, then we know the line is altered from time to time by some emphatic occurrence that startles its steadiness and sends it, the narrative heartbeat, shooting up—shooting high. High event.

But just what kind of event, or occurrence, would startle the cardiograph of narrative and cause it to jump? Jump and then resettle to continue the rhythmic beep of storytelling? The question has two components. Besides first considering the *nature* of the dramatic event, writers must secondly make sure their narratives are not so colored, do not become so distorted, by high events that they become something else, some other genre of story. But if a writer understands how to accomplish the latter—that is, if he renders the high incident in a way that retains the tone and integrity of literary fiction, then the issue of the former—what sort of event he can use— becomes easy: he can use anything. Death. Disappearance. Lust. Extravagant romance. All manner of mayhem and marvel and emotional extreme.

It is my experience that new writers make one of two mistakes when it comes to the use of high event. They either *(a)* include too little, if any at all, or *(b)*, as in the case of my student, include far too much. As for the first—the avoidance of high event—it's my hunch that many beginning writers carry the false idea that what distinguishes serious from commercial fiction is the absence of such moments in stories and novels. They think the one key thing that lifts storytelling out of the gutter of base tale is a kind of Puritan refusal to consider such tawdry devices—violence, suspense, titillation, and the like—in order to attract a discriminating reader.

This is an understandable misconception, one that some have said was encouraged at a certain point in time by the prototypical story in William Shawn's *New Yorker* at the height of its influence. Such a story was widely thought to be composed of tiny gestures and elliptical near-epiphanies; a story, as I once heard it defined, in which "nothing almost happens." Whether or not this was a fair perception, whether or not there was any validity to the notion of such a *New Yorker* prototype, it was, I think, a commonly held view, perhaps especially in MFA writing programs. And it may have helped suggest that if fiction was to be serious, to be literary, it had to be antiseptic in this way.

But such a restriction only exemplifies the worst sort of preciousness, conscious or not, in thinking about literature. And furthermore it punishes any writer who holds to it because it simply denies him or her some of storytelling's most valuable and available tools—the great assortment of high events.

Put slightly another way, I think many new writers sense that to give in, or give over, to including unapologetically dramatic moments in their stories is to sacrifice subtlety. The thinking goes that subtlety is a defining characteristic of serious fiction, and high drama, implying overly charged spectacle, is anomalous to subtlety. So if, as a writer, one wishes to tell a story subtly, one must ban these raucous barbarians—catastrophes, wild calamities, thrilling seductions, and so on—from the premises.

Certainly subtlety is a characteristic of serious fiction. But recognizing this basic truth should in no way prohibit the inclusion of high events. In fact, in serious fiction, the two go hand in hand. The very thing which makes high events possible, desirable, palatable *is* an accompanying subtlety which shapes the way they are presented. Indeed, the inclusion of a high or dramatic moment not only permits but requires the writer to bring a particularly great share of subtlety to bear on his fictional universe.

The issue, then, becomes how to apply that subtlety.

I suspect some of the confusion also has to do with mistaking the idea of subtlety for what amounts almost to lassitude, or at least quietude; extreme tranquility. Mistaking subtlety for inactivity. But in fact, the two have nothing in common. Rather, turning again to the trusty *Oxford English Dictionary*, subtlety is defined as "Acuteness, sagacity, penetration: in modern use chiefly with implication of delicate or keen *perception* of fine distinctions or nice points" (italics mine).

So subtlety is most definitely an essential quality of literary fiction, but it has much less to do with behavior, per se, than with how that behavior is perceived by the writer, and subsequently presented to the reader. To emphasize by example, I would argue, according to what is truly meant by literary subtlety, that such rambunctious works as *Catch-22* and *Portnoy's Complaint*, to offer a couple of random illustrations from contemporary literature, are helped to succeed by their interwoven subtlety.

If we think of readers, reading slick, commercial fiction on the one hand, and literary fiction on the other, it seems to me that when they read the former their motivating interest can be represented, as I have said, by their asking themselves, "What happens next? What happens next?" While, when they read the latter, the series of questions they ask are closer to this: first of all, yes, of course, "What happens?" But then, "In what way is that one event still happening?" And then, "How is it, now, continuing to happen?" And, "How is it happening still?" "And now?" Readers of literary fiction respond to the continuing call of one thing, or a few things, rather than to the easily and carelessly digested sequence of many things.

There is an absolute bond of cause and effect between reader and story that gets activated with the appearance of high events. This relationship can be illustrated if we think of the reader as a kind of spectator, or onlooker, who instinctively steps closer and pays greater attention when the narrative's even, steady tone is interrupted by the appearance of some animated or tumultuous or, in some other way, dramatically powerful incident. Thinking about this for even a moment, it only makes sense.

Imagine the reader/onlooker. She's standing at a bus stop on a busy city street at the end-of-the-day rush hour. She's waiting for her bus, periodically glancing down the avenue as the cars and taxis pass in their routine way at their routine pace. She feels this flow of traffic. In some engaged but unchallenging way she pays attention to it. But it's all comfortingly recognizable to her—the street and its buildings, the people gathered at the bus stop, the rhythmic speed and sound. Yes, she's watching this scene, which is to say, in this analogy, she's "reading" it. But she also keeps her natural, passively observational distance from it.

Then, during a momentary break in the traffic, she notices out of the corner of her eye a man leaving the huddle of those waiting for the bus and darting out into the street, hurrying to the other side. The man is halfway across the street when, as the speeding cars bear down, he stumbles, falls, and lies there helplessly as a mad, wild screeching of brakes fills the air.

I won't belabor the obvious. We can all visualize the reader/onlooker, jarred from her state of easeful attention to an immediately raised intensity of interest. And so it goes with narrative high event, which catches the reader as she "watches" the story—the lullingly familiar traffic moving by—then seizes her and causes her to pay much closer attention as catastrophe (or, though not in this depiction, some positive opposite) suddenly appears.

Effective narrative varies its pace, as the writer swiftly summarizes the story and alternately pauses to make a scene, for which he must slow down in order to inspect closely and report the details. As we have seen, dialogue is one device that slows the narrative in this way, and so, just as powerfully, does high event. I want to be sure it's clear what is meant when I speak of a narrative speeding up and slowing down. I certainly do not mean that readers receive and digest a dramatic moment with relative slowness. On the contrary, chances are better than very good that reading speed accelerates as the reader's interest is more closely summoned.

Instead, I am referring to the "distance," if you will, that any narrative must travel as it steps off, with whatever is its version of *Once upon a time*, and proceeds along toward its final destination—the conclusion of the story. It is in this sense of thinking of a narrative "moving," or traveling, that we recognize it slowing down when it happens on an event. It becomes less concerned about its linear progress toward *The End* (summary would obviously get it there more swiftly), than with delving deeply into the situation at hand.

Or, amplifying the concept slightly, think of it this way: again picture the narrative moving horizontally through the territory that is its story, the image I began with when I alluded to narrative as the line on a heart monitor. And then think of it, at strategic moments, pausing in its horizontal progress to change direction and ascend or descend vertically at instances of more elaborate scene-making.

The inclusion of event is extremely helpful as a way to achieve this quite necessary variety of pace and direction and attention as the reader/onlooker's relationship to a narrative intensifies and relaxes, sometimes staying observationally distant, sometimes coming closer for a more complete scrutiny.

How can high events be most effectively rendered? This question gets us centrally to that essential ingredient of subtlety, where we began by observing that in literary fiction subtlety was a matter of how dramatic behavior was perceived by the writer and then presented to the reader.

A by no means complete list of the ways subtlety can be achieved would include:

1. Describing violence in a counterintuitive tone, whether it be one of romance or myth or comic action or some other.
2. Directing the narrative circuitously, seemingly even casually, toward the high event, garnering a kind of momentum of obliqueness by insisting readers first attend to the details or the consequences before they encounter the moment which produced them.
3. Strategically placing the high event itself at the very edge of the narrative's frame of vision, maybe even entirely outside of it.

A Counterintuitive Tone

The first method can be shown in the beginning of Alice McDermott's novel *That Night*, first encountered in the chapter "Openings." Here McDermott immediately sets the tone and narrative point of view as she describes the story's high event—the fight between the local hoods, friends of Rick's, and the ad hoc army of husbands who feel called to defend their women and their turf:

> That night, when he came to claim her, he stood on the short lawn before her house, his knees bent, his fists driven into his thighs, and bellowed her name with such passion that even the friends who surrounded him, who had come to support him, to drag her from the house, to murder her family if they had to, let the chains they carried go limp in their hands. Even the men from our neighborhood, in Bermuda shorts or chinos, white T-shirts and gray suit pants, with baseball bats and snow shovels held before them like rifles, even they paused in their rush to protect her: the good and the bad—the black-jacketed boys and the fathers in their light summer clothes—startled for that one moment before the fighting began by the terrible, piercing sound of his call.

We hear in this passage, through the use of repetition and the lovely rolling cadence of the prose, an elevating tone that suggests the high event has become the stuff of lore in the narrator's memory. What was, in simplest reality, a plain and clumsy collision, is given, by the sound of the language, the sheen of nearly mythic battle.

Enforcing this impression, there is of course the fact that "that night" is remembered at all, and remembered in such detail, and with such audible fondness. Right away, McDermott establishes a pattern of recurrence that continues throughout the book as the narrator returns again and again to examine *that night* from various perspectives. In fact, the very phrase becomes a kind of lyric mantra as the novel proceeds. So the narrative stuff of the entire novel is made up of what permeates from just one high event that readers experience in the opening few pages of the book.

The sense of lore is further enhanced by the perceptions the narrator assigns to herself at the time of the event, when she was a typically impressionable young girl, ready to put a romantic cast on anything and everything, one who has monitored the thrilling teenage courtship as it has unfolded across the street and whose "ten-year-old heart"—as she watches the warring parties about to attack each other—"was stopped by the beauty of it all."

An even deeper sense of the mood and atmosphere develops on the next pages when the narrator remembers—and defends her memory—that only Venus, goddess of love, was shining brightly on "that night." The point again, to emphasize, is that we are out of the realm of explicit hand-to-hand bloodiness here, and into the altering disposition of myth. And when her narrator describes the fight itself, McDermott does something especially skillful as a way of giving us an indirect perception of the event transpiring:

> Until then, I had thought all violence was swift and sure-footed, somehow sleek, even elegant. I was surprised to see how poor it really was, how laborious and hulking. . . . There were no clever D'Artagnan mid-air meetings of chain and snow shovel, no eye-to-eye throat grippings, no witty retorts and well-timed dodges, no winners.

What McDermott accomplishes here is both a debunking of the notion of violence as something bloodlessly graceful while, by employing the very language of that notion—"swift and surefooted, sleek and elegant," "clever D'Artagnan mid-air meetings," "witty retorts"—she puts the imagery of a kind of urbane battle in our minds. She tells us that in reality the fight was a dumb and artless thing, nobody at all skilled at inflicting harm. So the reader is directed away from any details of pain and injury, both by the impression that the combatants were woefully ineffectual, but also by the contradictory language of a stylized *Three Musketeers* choreography.

Then, giving a final emphasis, the narrator suggests the scene's raw romantic power moving out in waves that even swept up the early-middle-aged suburban mothers watching it, whose voices (in calling to their husbands) "had begun to echo, even take up that lovesick boy's bitter cry."

A Circuitously Directed Narrative

A second way of subtly rendering a high event, quite unlike McDermott's in *That Night* and equally effective in establishing indirection, can be found in Toni Morrison's *Sula*. A key dramatic moment occurs about halfway through the novel when Sula's best friend, Nel, walks in on her husband, Jude, as he and Sula engage in a marvelously primitive act of sexual foreplay.

A funny woman, [Jude] thought, not that bad-looking. But he could see why [Sula] wasn't married; she stirred a man's mind maybe, but not his body.

He left his tie. The one with the scriggly yellow lines running lopsided across the dark-blue field. It hung over the top of the closet door pointing steadily downward while it waited with every confidence for Jude to return.

Could he be gone if his tie is still here? He will remember it and come back and then she would . . . uh. Then she could . . . tell him. Sit down quietly and tell him. "But Jude," she would say, you *knew* me . . . So how could you leave me when you *knew* me? . . .

But they had been down on all fours naked . . . like dogs . . . and when I opened the door they didn't even look for a minute and I thought the reason they are not looking up is because they are not doing that . . . But then they did look up. Or you did. You did, Jude. And if only you had not looked at me the way the soldiers did on the train, the way you look at the children when they come in while you are listening to Gabriel Heater and break your train of thought . . . And finally you just got up and started putting on your clothes . . . and you buckled your pants belt but forgot to button the fly and she was sitting on the bed not even bothering to put on her clothes because actually she didn't need to because somehow she didn't look naked to me, only you did . . . [the bedroom] so shambly, and maybe it was that way all along but it would have been better if I had gotten the dust out from under the bed because I was ashamed of it . . . And then you walked past me saying, "I'll be back for my things." And you did but you left your tie.

Morrison structures a kind of three-step entrance to the dramatic moment, each step a tangential detour as the narrative meanders relentlessly toward the incident.

First, we are in Jude's mind as he thinks to himself that Sula might "stir a man's mind, but not his body." A statement that leads readers in a direction they quickly discover is very much the wrong one.

From there, Morrison's narrative focuses tightly on the pitiful detail of the necktie and again we scramble to locate ourselves. We discover that we are now in Nel's mind, after the event, as she ponders bits and pieces of the result—Jude's leaving. Note again that all of this comes before we even get to the incident. It's a perfect instance of the effect being explicit, the high event implicit, as readers are offered various places to stop and look, for their attentions to center—in Jude's mind, in the empty bedroom—while the telling makes its awful leisurely way toward its destination.

And when the event is at last reached—Jude and Sula naked, on all fours, on the floor—readers find that even now they remain in Nel's mind and that she, by strongly denying to herself just what she is seeing, consequently denies readers a straight-on view as well. We have been graphically told in the opening sentence of the paragraph what Nel is in fact beholding, but then Nel as narrator veers self-protectively away, far from the evidence so horribly before her, to a particularly frightening experience from her childhood: "if only you [i.e., Jude] had not looked up at me the way the soldiers did on the train"; and to small domestic moments with Jude: "if only you had not looked at me . . . the way you look at the children when they come in while you are listening to Gabriel Heater."

Finally, Nel's denial reaches a point of such heartbreaking desperation that it fixes on details that cause her poignant embarrassment, one that she feels for Jude because he's not noticed his fly is open, and shame also for herself because her bedroom looks so unkempt. Her inability or refusal to see what is before her has reached bottom and she is looking at the event through alien eyes. Even, the narrative suggests, to some degree through Sula's coldly assessing eyes.

So, in all these ways, the narrative attention in this passage in *Sula* is only glancingly and indirectly on the high event itself. Indirectly, and very effectively, and—given the shocked, numbed mind that is telling us about it—from a distorted point of vantage that is keenly representative of Nel's psychological state.

The Placement of High Event outside the Narrative Frame

In his story "Emergency," Denis Johnson uses elements of indirection found in both McDermott and Morrison, while adding another:

Around 3:30 A.M. a guy with a knife in his eye came in, led by Georgie.

"I hope *you* didn't do that to him," Nurse said.

"Me?" Georgie said. "No. He was like this."

"My wife did it," the man said. The blade was buried to the hilt in the outside corner of his left eye. It was a hunting knife kind of thing.

Nurse peered at him. "We'd better get you lying down."

"Okay, I'm certainly ready for something like that," the man said.

"I guess I'd better get the doctor," I said.

"There you go," Nurse agreed.

They got him lying down, and Georgie says to the patient, "Name?"

"Terence Weber."

"Your face is dark. I can't see what you're saying."

"Georgie," I said.

"What are you saying, man? I can't see."

Nurse came over, and Georgie said to her, "His face is dark."

Nurse went to the wall intercom and buzzed the doctor on duty, the Family Service person. "Got a surprise for you," she said over the intercom.

[The doctor] peeked into the trauma room and saw the situation: the clerk—that is, me—standing next to the orderly, Georgie, both of us on drugs, looking down at a patient with a knife sticking up out of his face.

"What seems to be the trouble?" he said.

Johnson seems to be immediately directing our attention to the core of the event: "Around 3:30 A.M., a guy with a knife in his eye came in." There's certainly no meandering, no three-step circling, à la *Sula*, here. But actually, the violent act itself—a wife stabbing her husband in the eye—has taken place before the story begins, so technically we are not confronted with the act itself, but rather with its result. We are not, that is, witness to the initiating high event, but instead to what we might think of as the subsequent one: "a guy with a knife in his eye came in . . ."

Nevertheless, if not the *highest* event, it's a hell of a memorable entrance.

Johnson's narrator, after plainly and sparely describing the patient's appearance, refuses to offer the reader any sensory details of blood, anguish, man-in-shock behavior, thereby creating the same diffusing effect as we read in the passages from McDermott and Morrison. Like Nel in *Sula*, Johnson's narrator is, for very different reasons, also not "looking," certainly not directly, explicitly, at the drama. Or at least he's not absorbing and objectively reporting it. Otherwise we would have *some* sensory information, and we don't.

Too, as with Nel's self-denying account, Johnson's narrator's is also true to the thoughts and reactions of his character, in this case one who is on drugs, a state of mind humorously audible in the story's dumb, disembodied tenor.

And by employing this flat comic narrative, Johnson brings to bear two human attitudes—the absence of emotion and deadpan humor—which we tend to think of as inherently contradictory to ways one might react to the evidence of violence. *Tone*, then, helps Johnson achieve a necessary refraction, just as it helped McDermott, whose prose, with its sweep and heated temperature, struck a quite dissimilar one.

Finally, when the wounded patient is led away to another part of the hospital, the comedy is further raised as those whose roles are to treat (or mistreat) him remain to consider matters of exclusive self-interest.

The doctor gathered the three of us around him in the office and said . . . "We've got to get a team here, an entire team. I want a good eye man. A great eye man. The best eye man. I want a brain surgeon. And I want a really good gas man, get me a genius. I'm not touching this one. I know my limits. We'll just get him prepped and sit tight. Orderly?"

"Do you mean me?" Georgie said. "Should I get him prepped?"

"Is this a hospital?" the doctor asked . . . "Are you the orderly?"

Georgie could be heard across the hall . . . singing a Neil Young song . . .

"That person is not right, not at all, not one bit," the doctor said.

"As long as my instructions are audible to him it doesn't concern me," Nurse insisted . . . "I've got my own life and the protection of my family to think of."

The eye man was on vacation or something. While the hospital's operator called around to find someone else just as good, the other specialists were hurrying through the night to join us. I stood around looking at charts and chewing up more of Georgie's pills . . . Various nurses, and two physicians who'd been tending somebody in I.C.U., were hanging out down here with us now.

Everybody had a different idea about exactly how to approach the problem of removing the knife from Terrence Weber's brain. But when Georgie came in from prepping the patient . . . he seemed to be holding the hunting knife in his left hand.

Here again, the *consequences* hold explicit center stage, while the hapless Terence Weber, who embodies them, has left the room entirely. Until, with perfect timing, the narrator delivers the strategic punch line—the reentry of the whacked-out Georgie, holding the knife.

So, although they achieve their effects in highly individual way, all three works—*That Night, Sula,* and "Emergency"—have in common a focus on their events' repercussions, their surrounding ripples, rather than on the incidents themselves.

I relied on E. M. Forster in discussing the need for sympathetic characters, and I will quote him again, from *Aspects of the Novel:* "Incident springs out of character and, having occurred, it alters that character" (90). Equating Forster's "incident" with "high event," I have come to agree with only the first part of his statement. Certainly, incident, or event, does spring from character. Indeed, it is a major reason why a story needs events: to help define and clarify who each character is. But I am not sure that, as Forster says, incident always alters character. It seems to me that, more accurately, incident always temporarily engages and commands the full attention of a character, after which he or she may or may not be permanently altered. And a character who refuses or is somehow unable to change is surely every bit as interesting and intriguing as one who does.

I raise this issue with a particular character in mind—Peg, the wife and mother who discovers two dead bodies in Alice Munro's great story "Fits," a piece of work that—more emphatically than does Johnson's "Emergency"—places the high event outside the explicit narrative, its telling solely concerned with the aftereffects.

In "Fits," Peg, who has been married five years to Robert, is the mother of two teenage sons by a first marriage, and is living in one of the small Canadian towns that Munro has claimed as her terrain, takes some eggs to her next-door neighbors and finds them in their bedroom, dead of gunshot wounds. Here, obviously, is the story's most dramatic moment, and it is alluded to in the opening line: "The two people who died were in their early sixties."

After that, Munro, certainly aware that to begin with this information is to tap a reader's curiosity, moves away from it for several paragraphs, allowing it to percolate in our brains all the while. When the story next comes around to the incident, it is again a quick, one-sentence brushing by—"It was entirely by accident that Peg was the one who found them"(108)— after which it's off again to speak of Peg and Robert and who they are as individuals.

Finally, six pages into the story, it concedes—a word I use in admiration—to take us step-by-step through Peg's discovery. It is explained, however, not by Peg, but via a partly official, partly informal account that Robert has pieced together after reading the constable's report and talking to Peg. In other words, even now we do not hear from her, the character whose event it is, except indirectly.

In this fashion, Munro incrementally builds and complicates the story's more central interest, which is not the brutal shotgun deaths of the neighbors, but the great mystery of Peg's apparently unaffected behavior in the aftermath. It is this rippling-out of her eerie equanimity—variously unsettling to her sons, her friend at work, and, most of all, to Robert—that drives the story. Baffled by her seeming calm, one of her sons begins to remember his violent fantasies, when Peg and her first husband argued in front of him, that one of them was going to kill him. While Robert begins to remember an ugly affair with a woman, before he met Peg, which ended in a vicious argument that had him and his lover "trembling with murderous pleasure." And further on, Robert, his thinking infected by Peg's bemusing muteness, realizes that he hadn't thought to ask Peg about her "violent first marriage . . . til now."

There are additional examples, but they all underscore the

instrumental point: the great propulsion that results from a narrative strategy that repeatedly offers subtle echoes as opposed to a single simplistic shout. And nothing illustrates this better than Munro's masterful ending—which we will take up further in Chapter 7, "Closings"—with its startling revelation: that Peg had not been surprised by the bloody scene. She had known what she was walking into, and chose to, nevertheless:

> At noon, when the constable in the diner was giving his account, he had described how the force of the shot threw Walter Weeble backward. "It blasted him partways out of the room. His head was laying out in the hall. What was left of it was laying out in the hall."
> Not a leg. Not the indicative leg, whole and decent in its trousers, the shod foot. That was not what anybody turning at the top of the stairs would see and would have to step over, step through, in order to go into the bedroom and look at the rest of what was there. (131)

These last paragraphs are made doubly effective by their syntax, which is cast in the negative, giving readers even this most crucial information indirectly:

> the constable . . . described how the force of the shot threw [the neighbor] backward. "It blasted him partways out of the room. His head was laying out in the hall. What was left of it was laying out in the hall."
> *Not* a leg. [Which is what Peg told Robert she first saw.] *Not* the indicative leg, whole and decent in its trousers, the shod foot. That was *not* what anybody turning at the top of the stairs would see and would have to step over, step through, in order to go into the bedroom and look at the rest of what was there.

In both its overall design and its closest inspections, Munro's story implicitly tells us what Peg saw by explicitly telling us what she did not see. So much more powerful, because so much more allusive and lingering.

Having started this discussion by disagreeing with Forster, I wonder at this point if he is right after all in saying that the character is always altered by the primary incident. Couldn't it be argued that Robert, not Peg, is the central character in "Fits"? If you consider who in the story has the most to learn, who is most vulnerable to the consequences of the event, who, in short, has the most at stake, then Robert certainly qualifies. In any case, it is Robert whom we leave at the moment of stunned recognition, and we can only speculate on what will come to pass between him and Peg, a resolution—how perfect—that is due to take place outside the realm of story that readers have direct access to.

A few years ago in Cambridge, Massachusetts, an MIT student, who had come to the school from his native Sweden, was walking late at night across a Charles River bridge when a group of high school boys jumped him and stabbed him to death. There was, as would be expected, a great, if brief, reaction of horror to this unfathomable crime and, as I recall, a lot of discussion about the all-too-characteristic violence of American, as compared with Swedish, culture.

When a reporter went to the boys' high school and asked several of their fellow students what they thought and felt, the general response was that it was of course horrible that such a thing had happened, but no one should be too shocked or surprised because, nowadays, this sort of violence "happens all the time."

Well, as a matter of fact, in real life, this sort of violence, *with no accompanying long-lasting emotional consequence,* does not happen all the time. Where it happens all the time is on television and in the way television news is presented and, of course, in mainstream commercial movies: Michael Douglas, he and his family having been systematically terrorized by an insane Glenn Close, finally succeeds in killing her—about three times—in the bathtub. After which he puts his arm around Ann Archer, the wife he has betrayed, and they walk smiling arm-in-arm into the house, a kind of, "Whew, rough day. Let's celebrate. How about that great little Italian place we used to go to?" mood to it all.

I do not in any way claim an original perception when I say that in our culture, the enveloping images of "chaos and calamity and cut to the commercial of the family made happy by their new SUV," such images have effected a kind of brainwashing. Or if not that then at least an enormous misperception that, "nowadays," people shrug off every manner of traumatic event, "because it happens all the time."

The relevant point, as it applies to literary fiction writing, is my sense, based on talking with new writers, that some of them treat dramatic events so cavalierly, piling them up, heedless of an inventory, because they believe that it is the way to capture not only a reader's attention, but also some sort of narrative verisimilitude. But in truth, if a writer wishes to work and refine his fiction to reflect the texture of real life, he should keep in mind the fact that, in life, people react to keenly dramatic instances—whether horror or grief or high sublimity— with a sudden and profound emotional jolt (the cardiograph spiking to a frantic, jagged peak), after which the experience continues for quite some time, continuously redefined, refracted, mutedly pulsing, and still very much alive.

This is essential for us to keep in mind as writers; and at least as important to keep in mind as citizens. Maybe it's the long half-life of sorrow. Maybe the aftertaste of celebration. Choose your metaphor. But somehow remember that schlock is primarily interested in the breathless depiction of the drama.

While literary fiction is interested in the richness of the resonance. And because that resonance is the true condition of the world, it should also be true of the worlds we make in fiction. Our lives, if we let them, can advise us on our art.

6

Sentiment versus Sentimentality

The First, Always; the Second, Never

I take it for granted that every serious writer recognizes the reprehensibility of sentimental prose. I'm making this assumption in part because I have never heard a student voice anything other than concern or dismay or even more extreme despair when I've pointed out to him some aspect of his work that was sentimental. Never has one reacted in a way that would suggest he believes there is an argument to be made for sentimentality. But just in case, let's be clear that, by dictionary definition, sentimentality is the "affectation of sensibility, exaggerated insistence upon the claims of sentiment." And I particularly want to underscore the latter phrase—*the exaggerated insistence upon the claims of sentiment*—as we distinguish between sentimentality, on one hand, and sentiment on the other, and examine ways in which writers can "insist" on the infusion of sentiment in their stories while making certain that insistence does not become "exaggerated."

Some of the difficulty in separating sentiment from sentimentality, of embracing the former and rejecting the latter, has to do with the fact that they are not opposites. Rather, as the definition says, sentiment is contained in sentimentality. Sentimentality is sentiment run amok. It's as if a tree, the sentiment tree, were in one case kept artfully trimmed and shaped, and in another allowed to grow untended until its branches overwhelmed all the others in the orchard, killing the grass because no sun could penetrate the canopy of leaves and producing lousy fruit because the limbs were never pruned.

John Gardner's thoughts are instructive in making the necessary distinction. "Sentimentality," he wrote, in *The Art of Fiction*, "is the attempt to get some effect without providing due cause . . . [it is] emotion or feeling that rings false, usually because achieved by some form of cheating or" —again the word—"exaggeration."

So there is not only a fundamental aesthetic objection to sentimentality, but an equally unwelcome ethical one. It is a matter of either cheating, as Gardner says, in order to draw the desired emotional response from a reader; or, in the case of sentiment, of employing the tools and devices of narrative with a touch of deft legitimacy. (Which is not to say that sentiment does not involve a certain manipulation of the reader. I think manipulation, per se, is neither unethical nor inartistic. A central ambition of storytelling is to inspire the response in readers that you, the writer, are aiming for. But what is at issue is the means by which we achieve that response. The manner in which we manipulate the reader. Fairly, so that the response resonates? Or "by some form of cheating"?)

In her contributory essay to the anthology *Why I Write*, Joy Williams says, "Good writing never soothes or comforts. It is no prescription, neither is it diversionary, although it can and should enchant while it explodes in the reader's face." It may seem on first reading that Williams is describing an especially uncharitable art, detailing as she does all the things that good writing is not inclined to do. A sort of aesthetic tough love, should we as readers agree to the conditions. But actually that is not what Williams is saying at all. As she makes implicitly clear, she is speaking of the gratuitous gestures of commercial pap as opposed to serious writing's more intricate charity and echoing generosity. She's defining the kind of writing that requires the engagement of both our emotions and our intellect and, asking for this double commitment, rewards us doubly or, at the top of its form, exponentially.

The qualities that Williams identifies are at the same time exact and encompassing in suggesting the duties of worthy fiction. And even more fortuitous, she provides us with an invaluable checklist that we can use to make sure our work stays free of sentimentality. It seems, then, an especially good idea to isolate her terms, indeed make a literal list of them to keep close at hand as we proceed.

Good writing, writing that is free of sentimentality but infused with sentiment,

> Does not soothe or comfort
> Does not prescribe
> Does not simply divert
> Should enchant
> Should explode in the reader's face

(I salute her distinction between diversion and enchantment. The latter, it seems to me, requires charm, captivation that touches the mind and the senses. Diversion can be accomplished crudely. You can make a noise, turn on a light, if all you need to do is divert someone's attention, but you need to enchant him if wish to hold it.)

If writing of merit involves both our emotions and our intellect, we can combine the first three items on the list— doesn't soothe or comfort, prescribe, or divert—to make the point that sentimentality is by its nature simplistic, inviting readers to surrender the intellectual, the mindful, aspect of their makeups. For don't we soothe or comfort someone by saying, in effect, There, there, don't think about it? Don't we prescribe or divert by saying to our listener, Forget what's on your mind. Listen to this. Look over here? In other words, aren't we saying in each case, Don't think?

Actually, sentimentality goes beyond the invitation to surrender one's intellect; it *relies* on it in order to accomplish its effect, which is, if momentarily powerful, inevitably ephemeral. Because sentimental writing exclusively targets the visceral, the membrane of pure feeling, forever ready to be touched and agitated.

But, one might say, what's wrong with that? What's wrong with pure sensation? Isn't that what stories are supposed to do? Inspire us to emote? To stir and to move us? Aren't they supposed to take aim at our hearts?

Well, yes, I would argue that this is indeed *part* of what stories are supposed to do. The problem is that sentimentality aspires only to that, or (if the writer is after something more and does not recognize the tone he has created) *achieves* only that.

As opposed to fiction of shallow scheme and fleeting impact, serious writing is distinguished by its complexity. Complexity; complicatedness; which has nothing in common with confusion. I have made this point with different emphases in earlier chapters, saying that, without complexity, the telling merely glides along the unabrasive surface of schlock narrative. That without complexity, the characters we create, both major and minor, are unconvincing monotones of goodness and evil. And that without complexity, the dramatic events in the stories we write evaporate without a lingering whiff of aftereffect and consequence.

If you think about it for a moment, it becomes obvious that sentimentality is a contributing culprit in all this. In the matter of narrative, sentimentality hasn't the intelligence to pause or the capacity to delve. To linger over a moment would be to risk inspection, and its insubstantiality would be quickly exposed. Like a shark, sentimental writing must move constantly and compulsively through the waters of narrative in order to keep its pulse going.

Neither does sentimentality have the vision to take in the messiness that marks real life and, therefore, convincing stories. Being blind to the litter and irresolutions of the world, sentimentality insists instead on an obsessive tidiness as it gathers up the threads of story and joins them in neatly tied bows of contrived conclusion.

And with regard to characters and the dramas they incur, sentimentality forces on us monotypical extremes of the angelic and the diabolical, which it must have in order to create a pitch of tragic scream or joyful noise when the heavenly and demonic forces collide.

But, one might say, isn't it the goal of the storyteller to evoke a world so compelling and credible that readers are willing, as the phrase goes, to suspend their disbelief and eagerly enter it? Isn't that what John Gardner had in mind when he wrote that writers must strive to create worlds that readers experience as uninterrupted dreams?

Yes, to the first question; no, to the second. It is true that the aim is to talk the reader through the antechambers of skepticism and to get him to step without his noticing through the portal that leads from his real world into your invented one. But suspending disbelief does not mean surrendering the wish or the need to reason. It is instead a matter of the reader leaving one universe, his actual life, where thought and analysis and rumination are required, for an alternate one where they are needed just as much. Isn't it the case that your dreams, while you are in them, propel you through narratives that you are continuously challenged to make sense—not merely sensation—of?

In the title essay of her collection *The End of the Novel of Love*, Vivian Gornick writes that, after finishing Jane Smiley's novella *The Age of Grief* and feeling real but finally modest admiration for it, she asked herself, "Why [is this story] only a small, good thing? Why am I not stirred to a sense of larger things here? Almost immediately I answered myself with, Love is the problem here. It's the wrong catalyst. It doesn't complicate the issue. It reduces it" (155).

I cite this passage not to argue that love is, perforce, sentimental. I do not believe it is, and that is not what Gornick is saying. But reading it, I was struck by the applicability of her last two sentences—*It doesn't complicate the issue. It reduces it*—to the behavior of sentimental writing.

It is worth repeating: Sentimentality never complicates the issue. It always reduces it. Hence, sentimental prose has no power to pervade and hence has no possibility, in Gornick's words, to stir us "to a sense of larger things."

Further on in the same essay, Gornick writes, in a similar vein, "When a novel gives us less than many of us know—and is content with what is being given—we have middlebrow writing [that] is closer to the sentimental than to the real."

Exactly so. The besetting sin of sentimentality is that it functions to minimalize and trivialize, never to deepen, any given moment in which it exerts its influence.

If it is clear that sentimentality is to be avoided, how can we hope to suffuse our work with a quality of sentiment that does not become exaggerated? In answer, remembering again the list fashioned from Joy Williams's definition of good writing, I would emphasize two requirements—*rigorous descriptive precision* and equally a *relentless restraint*—that result in writing that has the chance to enchant readers and explode in their faces. Both precision and restraint contribute to a kind of *leavening* of the sentiment, a tempering that is necessary in order to keep it from becoming extreme.

John Cheever's story "The Cure" beautifully illustrates the

characteristics of narrative precision and restraint. It is one of Cheever's classic portraits of life in exurban New York, that country of rueful courtesies and decorous longing he made singularly his. The story begins with the narrator telling us,

> My wife and I had a quarrel and Rachel took the children and drove off in the station wagon. . . . She had left me twice before—the second time we had divorced and then remarried—and I watched her go each time with a feeling that was far from happy, but also with that renewal of self-respect, or nerve, that seems to be the reward for accepting a painful truth. As I say, it was summer, and I was glad in a way, that she had picked this time to quarrel. It seemed to spare us both the immediate necessity of legalizing our separation. We had lived together—on and off—for thirteen years; we had three children and some involved finances. I guessed that she was content, as I was, to let things ride until September or October.
>
> I was glad the separation took place in the summer because my job is most exacting at that time of year and I'm usually too tired to think of anything else at night and because I'd noticed that summer was for me the easiest season of the year to live through alone. I also expected that Rachel would get the house when our affairs were settled and I like our house and thought of those days as the last I would spend there.

We immediately hear in the narrator's account a tone of extraordinary, even eerie dispassion that is at odds, to say the least, with the circumstances he's describing. He presumes his marriage is ending, that his children will be taken from him, that he will be forced to leave the comfort and history of his house, and yet he offers all this to us in a voice of resoundingly practical detachment. I particularly admire Cheever's use of the pallid and almost offhand-seeming "glad," with which the narrator twice characterizes his feelings about his wife's choice of summer as the season for her departure. *Glad?* we think. He may as well be confirming a Sunday morning tee time. *Oh, good, I'm glad it's ten. That'll leave me time to clean out the garage.*

This very mismatch of events and the abandoned husband's apparent attitude toward them conveys not the absence, but the nearly palpable denial of emotion. In other words, feeling, sentiment, is very much present from the outset, but thoroughly tamped down, creating a mood of disquieting emotional unreliability. We feel sentiment in these sentences not because it is displayed but because it is under such repressive pressure we can sense the struggle required to keep it from escaping. Were the narrator to launch his story with a wail, some high keening of distress, the tone might at first sound more recognizable and seem more understandable to us but would quickly lose its strength and interest simply because it was, in our reflexive predetermination of how these domestic traumas affect those involved, so much the sound we assumed we would hear. I do not believe it would produce the same energetic sentiment, the tension and curiosity, as does Cheever's narrative restraint, which he accomplishes by giving the husband a voice of discordant calm.

This voice, perfectly pitched, continues as the narrator explains his rational plan for passing the summer nights alone.

> The first months will be like a cure, I thought, and I scheduled my time with this in mind. I took the eight-ten train into town in the morning and returned on the six-thirty. I knew enough to avoid the empty house in summer dusk, and I drove directly from the station parking lot to a good restaurant called Orpheo's. . . . Afterward I'd drive over to the Stonybrook Drive-In Theatre and sit through a double feature.

Logical as his decisions may be, affectless as is the tone in which they are explained, we recognize in the motives behind them the emotional turmoil he is so determined to keep dormant. Furthermore, we begin to learn that he recognizes it, too. *I knew enough to avoid the empty house in summer dusk.* In other words, the texture of sentiment in the story is, with masterful subtlety, becoming gradually its surface as well as its substratum.

At this point the story takes a turn as the gathering strength of his loneliness and sorrow competes with his refusal to look directly at it. Waking in the night and unable to return to sleep, he goes downstairs to read. "Our living room is comfortable. The book seemed interesting." (The fiercely uninvested adjectives and reportorial flatness continue.) And then, after a few minutes,

> I heard, very close to me, a footstep and a cough. I felt my flesh get hard—you know the feeling—but didn't look up from my book, although I felt that I was being watched . . . Then a fear, much worse than the fear of the fool outside the window, distracted me. I was afraid that the cough and the step and the feeling I was being watched had come from my imagination. I looked up.
>
> I saw him all right, and I think he meant me to; he was grinning.

For the first time in the story real emotion (being "glad" earlier hardly counts) explicitly appears on the narrative surface. Not only does it appear, he labels it for us and in so doing acknowledges that it has appeared. More than that, he confesses that he wonders if he is hearing and seeing things, a deeper admission that what is going on inside him is considerably more turbulent than he's insisted.

But even after this initial revelation, the narrator redoubles his determination to assure us—and himself—that his summer isolation and the impending loss of his family are nothing he cannot absorb with equanimity. He willfully gives the Peeping Tom the sad and unthreatening face of an old man and manages "to think compassionately [of him,] driven, in senescence, to leave his home and wander at night in a strange neighborhood."

I will summarize the steady escalation of the narrator's emotional unraveling, which leads to two moments that, for me, "explode in the reader's face." First, he sees the Peeping Tom again the next night and, running to the window, calls out, "She's gone! Rachel's gone! There's nothing to see!" and thus in an inadvertent impromptu shout speaks directly of the preoccupying despair we have sensed from the beginning.

Through the following nights he continues to be unable to sleep. He decides one morning, upon seeing a neighbor and his family on the platform of the train station, that he, the neighbor, is the Peeping Tom. He dreams of a noose floating in the air. He begins to violate the strict terms of his cure, taking later trains to work, staying longer in the city, drinking more and more. The image of the floating noose continues to haunt him. At a cocktail party, he sees an aging but still beautiful actress of his acquaintance who gives him what he perceives to be "a sad, sad look," and who, on leaving, comes up to him, puts her hand on his arm and says, "You poor boy . . . You poor, poor boy." Her sympathy, he decides, is inspired by her belief that he will hang himself.

Then one afternoon, "anesthetized by gin" after a business lunch, he wanders into Brooks Brothers, where he sees a young woman. "Her arms and legs were beautiful, but the look on her face was sensible, humorous, even house-wifely, and this sensible air seemed to accentuate the beauty of her arms and legs." He follows her out of the store, walks beside her on the sidewalk. She senses him following her and he knows she does, but he is so lost in the misery that has by now taken hold of him that he flagrantly continues to trail her through the midday crowd, assuring himself that "she was the kind of woman who would not readily call for help." We can't fathom what he will say or do to her because it is rivetingly clear that he has no idea himself. Until while waiting with her at a corner for the light to change, he tells us,

> It was all I could do to keep from saying to her, very, very, softly, "Madame, will you please let me put my hand around your ankle? That's all I want to do, Madame. It will save my life." . . . She crossed the street and I stayed at her side, and all the time a voice inside my head was pleading, "Please let me put my hand around your ankle. It will save my life. I just want to put my hand around your ankle. I'll be very happy to pay you." I took out my wallet and pulled out some bills. Then I heard someone behind me calling my name. I recognized the hearty voice of an advertising salesman who is in and out of our office. I put the wallet back in my pocket, crossed the street, and tried to lose myself in the crowd.

Among the things that make this a moment of exploding sentiment, rather than sentimentality, I will point out two. First of all, the description of the woman, who has, yes, beautiful arms and legs, but who overall gives off a "sensible" and "house-wifely" air. She is not some ravishingly exotic creature of airbrushed perfection who turns grown men weak and stupid and bumping into one another as she walks by. She is attractive in a quiet and ordinary way and it is that very exemplary housewifeliness—that quality, we can infer, which makes her spectrally the wife who has left him—which stirs the narrator and leaves him pitifully at the mercy of his desire.

Second, the achingly humble and subservient nature of his

request. We do not hear some fantasized act of savage sex and conquest building in his mind. *I saw me taking her right there, in Brooks Brothers, on the floor beneath a row of 46 extra longs.* Instead, we get a more erotically charged, because more tangibly and mutedly strange, image. One that is at the same time somehow almost plausible and yet absolutely impossible. Pitiably timid and yet extremely creepy. A beaten man pleading and ready to pay for an act that is, by the clichéd measure of violation, hardly rapacious, but in its excruciating sadness (and comedy) somehow more intimate and so more violating.

And then the story's climax:

> I took the train home, but I was too tired to go to Orpheo's and then sit through a movie. I drove from the station to the house and put the car in the garage. . . . As soon as I stepped into the living room, I noticed on the wall some dirty hand prints that had been made by the children before they went away. They were near the baseboard and I had to get down on my knees to kiss them.

Invoking again those features of *restraint* and *precision* so essential to the success of this second explosive moment, notice that, while the act being described is highly dramatic, the teller's tone has not altered—and does not for a syllable through the entire story—from its introductory plainness. Even here, there is a casualness reverberating, as though he were saying he got down on his knees to plug in a light. Had the narrative volume somehow been raised and made artificially lush at this moment it would have resulted in two kinds of fatal harm. First, our attention would have turned from the action itself to the sound and stridency of the prose. Second, and connected to the first, the location of the feeling, the source of the sentiment, would have then resided not inside the character but outside, in the author imposing a heightened mood by turning up the dials. But as written, we sense, as we should, this final eruption to be a wholly organic one, coming to us from inside the character.

Further evidence of Cheever's restraint and precision in this story: the husband/father's release of despair is inspired by the most homely of sights—his children's (who in their absence or his memory of them have not once been directly mentioned) smudged handprints, something that under other circumstances would have likely gone unnoticed or even caused the narrator's annoyance. *Those damn kids, dirtying up the walls. What were they doing down there on the floor anyway?* In the unfortunate imagination of a sentimental writer, the provocation might have been the set of crutches uncovered in the garage, left from the time one of the children broke his leg. He might have discovered and kissed a favorite doll, mutilated by love, spotted as he gets down on his knees to retrieve some change that has rolled under the couch. The doll, the puppy, the baseball glove—these sorts of tokens, saccharine and generic, are sure signs that sentimentality has entered the building.

(As an aside, I can't help mentioning too the fact that, in kneeling down as he does, the narrator mimics the position he must have had in his mind as he fantasized touching the woman's ankle. I have no idea of course if this replication was intentional on Cheever's part, but there it is, brilliantly precise.)

Finally, listen carefully to how Cheever writes this key line: *I had to get down on my knees to kiss them.* There is sheer artistry in the calculation behind the phrasing of that sentence. It emphasizes not that he kissed the handprints but by what physical means he reached them and in that emphasis there is the implication that the action itself was obvious and inevitable. It is saying, in effect, *Of course I kissed my children's handprints. Nothing remarkable about that. You certainly would have too if you were feeling what I felt, and here is what I had to do to get to them.* He is in such a state by now that he doesn't presume his action to be the least noteworthy, to be anything other than the common one. But we find it noteworthy indeed, and the well-earned heartbreak this instant produces has to do with our recognizing that he has traversed a landscape that began with his determination to present a facade of emotional imperturbability, and has ended with his having so lost his grip that he is completely unaware of the impression he makes, of the degree to which he has revealed himself as he grovels in his need to kiss the dirt his children made.

The story ends in two last quick paragraphs. Later that night the phone rings and, intuitively knowing it is his wife, he answers in a burst of urgent love that's been kept so arduously contained for so long—"Oh, my darling! . . . I'll drive all night . . . I'll get there in the morning."

And then this final bit of information: "That was all . . . I packed a bag and turned off the icebox [even here, the marvelous precision of domesticity] and drove all night. We've been happy ever since . . . Everyone here is well."

Oh? Are they really? Or has he been able to refashion his veneer of emotional surety? We ask these questions, and continue to, as all great stories insist we do. We ask them in the case of "The Cure" because that veneer has been so convincingly conveyed, because the quality of sentiment has been precisely and with restraint braided through a dispatch from the heart of one of Cheever's inimitable principalities.

I said that I had never known someone to defend sentimentality as a positive feature in his or her work. But there have been times when it has been difficult to convince a new writer that the fiction under discussion *was* in fact sentimental. Usually that debate has focused on the disparity between the events in the story and how they ultimately come together, an incongruence between the astringent, tough-minded intelligence displayed throughout a story and the manner in which that story concludes. It seems, from this, that it may be easier for many new writers to spot a flaw in the way a character or incident is drawn, to hear an overheated or breathless or sappy tone, than to detect sentimentality in the overall blueprint.

The Grimms' fairy tale "Faithful John," the opening of which was rewritten in Chapter 2 to show several ways of beginning a story, is of real value at this juncture.

Again, the tale starts by telling us, "An old king fell sick; and when he found his end drawing near, he said, 'Let Faithful John come to me.'" John is the king's most loyal servant, and the king asks of him the sort of favor that could be posed to only the most loyal servant. He requests that John watch over his son, the source of his only remaining concern, and John agrees without hesitation to do so, "even [if] it should cost me my life." Not for nothing is he called Faithful John. The king says that's fine, he can now die in peace, but, oh, there is one thing he forgot to mention.

> [A]fter my death, show him the whole palace. . . ; but take care how you show him one room,—I mean the one where hangs the picture of the daughter of the king of the golden roof. If he sees it, he will fall deeply in love with her, and will then be plunged into great dangers on her account: guard him in this peril.

John gives no thought as to why the picture is hanging there in the first place, or, if it's so dangerous, why they don't just take it down now and throw it in the fire. He only reiterates his pledge to the king, the king again says thanks, lowers his head to his pillow, and dies.

Days of mourning follow, and then Faithful John says to the young new king that it is time to show him around the palace, and we all know what happens next. (We can envision John trying to hustle them past the forbidden door as the young king asks, "Hey, what's this room?" "Oh, that? Just a closet.")

When the young king coerces John to let him see what's in the room, he gazes up at the picture, faints, and, after being revived, insists that John take him to meet the beautiful princess with the idea of asking her to become his queen. This act of courtship first involves much melting down of the palace gold and casting it into the shapes of "birds, wild beasts and wonderful animals" to offer the princess, gold being her weakness. After that, there is a long boat trip to her island.

Once they have arrived, the young king tempts the princess on board to see all the gold, and while they are down below, Faithful John sits out on the deck, playing his flute. There he spots three ravens perched on a railing. They're talking among themselves in their own tongue, but unbeknownst to them John speaks fluent Raven and he hears them prophesying a series of events that threaten either to separate the lovers or cause one of them to die.

> After the wedding, when the dance begins, and the young queen dances on, she will turn pale, and fall as though she were dead; and if someone does not draw near and lift her up and take from her right breast three drops of blood, she will surely die. But if any one knew this, he would tell him, that if he does do so, his body will turn to stone, from the crown of his head to the tip of his toe.

Faithful John keeps his information to himself, and of course, back at the palace, the moment comes. The queen faints, John sweeps her up off the floor, lays her on a couch, and draws three drops of blood from her right breast. She immediately breathes again, but the young king has seen it all. He charges Faithful John with "boldness," which seems fairly lenient, all things considered, but which as it turns out carries the penalty of being hanged the next day.

I want to pause here to make a first point about sentiment versus sentimentality in this story. It is very easy, it's a cheap shot really, to tease the tale for its preposterous events and for the gaps in its plot. But more importantly, remember that this was a story written for children, and yet it is one—typically of the Grimms'—filled with vivid scenes of death and danger, allusive sex, complicated pledges of honor and seeming betrayal, all told in a strong, even, straightforward tone.

In other words, given that tone and the audience to which the story was directed, this is hardly a narrative that *soothes* and *comforts*. It may have flaws according to our contemporary sensibility but, in terms of its pitch and its moment-to-moment occurrences, sentimentality is so far not one of them.

The next morning, as John is about to be hanged, he confesses to the king why he behaved with such scandalous impertinence the night before, and the king calls out, "O my most faithful John! pardon! pardon! take him down!" But it is too late. Just as the ravens predicted, John turns instantly to stone.

The king and queen are horrified, weep deeply for their servant, and the king orders the stone figure of John taken up to his room and placed near his bed.

Life goes on, the queen bears two beloved children, but they continue to mourn the loss of John. One day, while the queen is at church, the king says to the statue, "O that I could bring thee back to life, my Faithful John!" And to his great surprise, the statue answers him, saying that, in fact, he can, if he will give up what is dearest to him. The king eagerly agrees and the statue says, "Then cut off the heads of thy children, sprinkle their blood over me, and I shall live again."

Amazing as is the statue's demand, more so is the king's only momentary hesitation as he remembers how John died for his sake. He raises his sword "to cut off his children's heads and sprinkle the stone with their blood, but the moment he drew [it] Faithful John was alive again."

We hear then that "the king was full of joy" and "the children sprang about." Now the king decides to trick the queen. He hides John and the children in a closet, and when the queen returns from church he tells her he has learned that they can bring John back to life if they kill their sons. She "turned pale and was frightened in her heart," but astonishingly and without pause she also agrees to the terms, because "we owe him all, for his great faith and truth." Her words delight the king, he opens the closet, John and the children rush out, the king explains his prank to the queen, and "all lived happily together the rest of their lives."

Certainly, from this summary, the point is already clear: that sentimentality has appeared with a vengeance at the end. An abruptly, implausibly joyous conclusion such as this one is another form of sentimentality. It is, as I said, not a matter of tone or specific incident. In "Faithful John," as we saw, there was a consistency of carefully presented drama throughout, building to the prospects of blood and horror that immediately preceded the happy finish. No, the problem is one of overall scheme—that happy finish itself—and the presence of sentimentality in this guise again demonstrates its appalling need to make things neat and tidy, to fashion infantile harmony from life's mature discord.

This style, you could say, of sentimentality has much in common with the problem discussed in Chapter 5, "High Events," where characters walk away from shattering trauma, whether catastrophic or ecstatic, completely unaffected by what they have just endured, their psyches and their pretty clothes unblemished. Furthermore, it is a tendency, not only in new writing, but one that is increasingly evident in much published fiction that is advertised and accepted as serious and literary.

The Grimms, after all, were working according to an established form, obliged to satisfy a set of inflexible expectations,
and writing in an era innocent of Freudian influence. But that
was then and this is now. They had reason and valid excuse for
enforcing a valedictory sentimentality at all cost. We do not.

And yet, as I said, sentimentality continues to spoil the
work of both those who are new to writing fiction and, with
ever greater frequency, those who aren't. In the case of inexperienced writers, as has been suggested, it's often the case of
not knowing what all to look for. In the second, it may be more
a matter of aesthetic laxness, perhaps a revised tolerance, some
redefined sensibility in these matters which allows the
entrance of sentimentality into the work. That is to say: insen-
sitivity to excessive sentiment.

It seems to me that there are two influential moods running
parallel in the culture. There's first of all the prevailing noise
of social incivility. It is a time in which sarcasm is understood
to be wit. We hear the tenor of this attitude everywhere. The
insulting put-down that has become the staple of TV sitcom
dialogue. The single note of mean glee in the rant of talk radio
America. And all this symptomatic of a general cynicism
whose passive stance is resignation, whose aggressive one is
irony.

Contrasting with that, and surely in response to it to some
degree, our aesthetic safe houses, our films and literature, to
which we have always retreated in order to gain perspective or
regain equilibrium, have gotten—invoking Joy Williams's list
once more—mindlessly soothing and comforting without
standards. The tales we are now often asked to read, desperate
to qualify as brave and happy ones, require a back story of safe
sadness that can be cleanly overcome. Whether this consciousness is presently so ingrained that it resides undetected
in us, or whether it is cynically offered—as in the case of polit-

ical discourse, where it is forever morning in America again and all those who run for office must publicly narrate a tear-jerking family tragedy—in either instance ours has come to be a culture that mistakes sentimentality for sincerity.

I proposed at the beginning that sentiment in fiction requires the presence of both intellect and feeling. Without intellect we have sentimentality. Without feeling we have formal puttering. Clearly those who write more experimental fiction that has no interest in the effort to represent "real life" feel in their admirable horror of sentimentality that any presence of emotion, any stir of feeling, is by definition a cheap, lesser art, aesthetic slumming. Given the alternative of sentimental emptiness, one has to be sympathetic to this view. But of course sentimentality need not *be* the alternative, and it seems to me that we as writers take a lesser risk if we resolve the problem of sentimentality threatening our art by inserting the V-chip of cold unbending irony.

What has gone so far unsaid is the obvious truth that the spirit of a culture and its aesthetic tastes evolve. The insistent final optimism, for example, in the work of Dickens, reads to us now as extremely sentimental, for all there is to admire in him. Similarly, the insistent final fatalism of Hardy. Our moral perspectives alter over time. The narrow polemic of Sinclair's *The Jungle*, the high melodrama of *Uncle Tom's Cabin*, send the siren screech of propaganda ringing in our ears. (Propaganda is always sentimental, and probably has to be.)

Maybe, with these shifts of sensibility in mind, part of the problem is that sentimentality is similar to pornography—the perception of it differing from person to person. Or, as the judge said, though you can't define it, you know it when you see—or read—it.

If this is so, then it might be helpful to think of it this way: Sentiment is to sentimentality as artful eroticism is to artless pornography. In each case, in the former both the mind and the senses are aroused. Consequently an impact is created that is earned and that lingers intricately, thoughts and urges intermingling. In the latter, the senses alone are touched, and the sensation disappears when the source is removed.

Sentiment is emotion that serves the scene. Sentimentality is emotion that dominates the scene.
Sentiment is selfless. Sentimentality is egomaniacal.
Sentiment—with reference to where we began—explodes. Sentimentality thickly oozes.
Sentiment charms. Sentimentality deceives.
Sentiment defines the dramatic instant. It adds to its dimension and refines its details. Sentimentality inflates the dramatic instant. All dimension, like a painted face on an overblown balloon, becomes distorted beyond recognition.

So if we have individual tolerances for how much feeling is too much, if our personal capacities for and indulgences in emotion vary considerably, one from another, we can each nevertheless monitor our work continuously as we compile and revise our personal list, one like the one I have just offered. We can define for ourselves what distinguishes these two qualities, sentiment as opposed to sentimentality, one of them vital, the other ruinous. We not only can do this, but if we wish to be serious about writing, we must.

7

Closings

Ways of Ending the Story

It only makes sense, if you think about it, that writers struggle as they face the question of how to end, because the challenge, in essence, is to find the words and the tone with which to say good-bye. This does not seem to me a sentimental analogy at all, for at base it is just what occurs at the conclusion of a work of fiction—the writer (or, more truly, the voice that is telling the story) saying good-bye to the reader. And we all know how difficult the moment of departure can be. Leaving a party, leaving a job, leaving a lover, leaving family and friends to move from Memphis to Chicago, we feel to varying degrees a dual desire to give a memorable parting impression while also wishing to stay true to who we are. We do not want our parting words to sound phony or awkward, to seem inappropriate to the nature of the relationship, but we do want them to have a keen impact. To ourselves, we can even admit that we hope they will linger.

And so it is with the endings of our stories.

As with most all elements of craft, the mistakes new writers make when they finish a story reflect the extremes of insufficiency or excess; too little or too much. In the first instance, the closing is depleted of energy and dissipates in a faint mumbling vagueness, as if the narrative has forgotten in midsentence its final train of thought. Either that, or, still full of energy, the story closes with an abrupt illogic, the reader figuratively lurching forward in the chair as the tale inexplicably slams on its brakes.

But just as often, a new writer's story laboriously concludes, sweatily exerting itself to make sure nothing has been left unexplained or subject to misinterpretation. Reading an ending of this latter sort, there comes to mind the image of someone putting up a tent and furiously hammering the anchoring pegs deep into the ground, then reaching for the extras he's brought along and starting in on them until he's secured a structure that could stand undisturbed against the gusts of hurricanes.

Unsuccessful closings are often written out of certain misguided assumptions, and I have often wondered, in the case of those that go on and on at dulling length, whether their writers believe the purpose of an ending is to "quiet" the story once and for all; to make certain that it has been pinned to the floor and successfully sedated.

I would say that any ending that succeeds both *culminates* and at the same time *continues* the story. The mix of these two factors naturally varies according to whether the writer's principal desire is, on one hand, to bring everything together, or, on the other, to leave matters more elliptically open. But both qualities, culmination and continuation, are fundamentally present.

When thinking of the manner in which a narrative behaves as it heads toward its ending, it might be valuable to equate it to a song sung in rounds. Opening with the quick clean phrases of establishing melody, the song—the story—builds and deepens, becoming steadily more complex, its gathering intricacy due to the staggered reintroductions of those first, initially unaccompanied phrases. Until the song/story reaches a point, the narrative line now at its densest, where the recurring phrases join and overlap for a fully interconnected and harmonious few moments—and what better definition of a plot reaching its climax?

After which, the flat-out volume again begins to fall and the harmony starts to simplify, the layers of participation—the elements of the plot—peeling away, leaving those last and once more solitary notes to be sung.

The metaphor is by no means perfect, but it can help us understand that the ending of a story is made up of, and relies on, all that has come before it. It gets its meaning and derives its relevance from the orchestrated strata of complexity that lead up to it. And in some fashion it repeats with a final echoing lucidity the essential strand of melody that was offered at the start.

The question, then, facing the writer is how to write an ending that benefits from all the complicated momentum that has been funneled into it; one that sounds its confidence and retains a narrower but still resounding power, even as it sings its final notes alone.

Staying with the premise that effective endings work both to culminate and continue the story, I want to look at some examples and make the idea plainer still by dividing them into two general classifications: those closings that strive to impart a sense of *summation;* and those that are in various ways deliberately more *partial.*

As always, and as was clearly the case when we gathered together models of the ways stories open, this process of broadly categorizing some element of fiction is a crude exercise at best, since the artful closing of a story or novel eludes firm definition.

There is a further handicap here, compared to a discussion

of openings, where we were at least able to read and experience them, even though they had been separated from the body of the story, pretty much as any reader would. We took up the story's opening as the story began; the first words we read were the first words there were.

Obviously, this is not the case with these biopsied closings, since the meaning, the full implication, of an ending is received; and the source of its energy is the very story it has been isolated from. But we can study them nevertheless and to good benefit. Think of them as stilled specimens pinned to a page, allowing us to examine their designs and, from that, their strategies.

The Closing of Summation

A closing that somehow conveys a sense of summary, inviting us to draw the inference that nothing of import has been overlooked, figuratively spreads its arms and collects the disparate parts and themes and characters and arranges them for a kind of final appearance. Of course, any closing that does only that is tedious and spiritless in the extreme.

John Gardner, with this sort of summarial ending in mind, speaks of the novel's need at the end to "return and repeat," the resummoning, the recalling, at the close, of the most significant moments that readers have encountered along the way.

But to make the point once more, it is not a matter of simply recalling these moments but of gathering them up in their apparent randomness and uniting them at the end by underscoring their connections. To use the image of the curtain call suggested above, it is as though the narrator, the emcee of a variety show, urges all the performers back for one last bow; the closing as a kind of literary encore. And as they return he now points out to the audience how the elephant act relates to the Italian opera singer—the rough translation of the title of her aria is "Pachyderm"—and that the comedian told a joke involving a hippopotamus, another species of pachyderm, who speaks Italian.

This final revelation of influence and connection at the end of a story is what Gardner calls "an organized return of images," and Marilynne Robinson's novel, *Housekeeping,* closes with just such a scheme of orderly beauty. The narrator, Ruth, having succumbed to the influence of her guardian, her deeply, cripplingly eccentric Aunt Sylvie, and having joined her in a life of sad, nomadic isolation, imagines at the end of the book her only sibling, her sister Lucille, whose where-abouts are unknown, because Lucille, in adolescence, had fled Sylvie's bizarre ways to claim a conventionally stable life for herself.

Here, at the conclusion of the novel, is Ruth:

Or imagine Lucille in Boston, at a table in a restaurant, waiting for a friend . . . Her water glass has left two-thirds of a ring on the table, and she works at completing the circle with her thumbnail. Sylvie and I do not flounce in through the door . . . We do not sit down at the table next to hers and empty our pockets in a small damp heap in the middle of the table, and sort out the gum wrappers and ticket stubs, and add up the coins and dollar bills, and laugh and add them up again. My mother, likewise, is not there, and my grandmother in her house slippers and her pigtail wagging, and my grandfather, with his hair combed flat against his brow, does not examine the menu with studious interest. We are nowhere in Boston. However Lucille may look she will never find us there, or any trace or sign . . . No one watching this woman smear her initials in the steam on her water glass with her first finger, or slip cellophane packets of oyster crackers into her handbag for the seagulls, could know how her thoughts are thronged by our absence, or know how she does not watch, does not listen, does not wait, does not hope, and always for me and Sylvie.

First, and most obviously, note Ruth, the narrator, bringing back the characters for one last glimpsing. Lucille, about whom she muses inventively. Her mother, who committed suicide. Her grandmother, the first inheritor of Ruth and Lucille after their mother's death. Her grandfather, who'd died years before in a train accident.

Take a moment, too, to turn back to the beginning of *Housekeeping* in the "Openings" chapter and see how this closing complements it with almost perfect symmetry, a comparison that helps to make the additional point that a closing of summation, in its thorough purpose and composition, roughly equates to the fable or fairy-tale opening.

Reading Robinson's closing, both on its own and in relation to her novel's opening, it is hard to imagine a better example of a narrative achieving a sense of completion, of the circle of story coming closed. You can hear the swell of oracular argument as Ruth moves toward conclusion. But if this is so, it is essential to ask how the ending of *Housekeeping* is able to retain such an edgy resonance; how, in other words, Robinson so successfully avoids rendering it inert even as she creates an impression of entirety, the sense that, in conclusion, she has accounted for everyone and everything.

I think she accomplishes it, first of all, through the sensory concreteness of Ruth's speculations; no airy abstractions, but rather hard clean images: thumbnail in the water ring; crackers into a pocket (we hear the crinkling cellophane). And beyond that, Robinson infuses her closing with a certain nervous life by brilliantly recasting the terms of narrative at its end, and in doing so she counters a reader's instinctive expectations of the way narrative typically speaks. I mean by this that we are accustomed to hearing and reading descriptions of what the characters before us *are* doing, *are* thinking, *are* feeling, and so on. Our picture of them in their moment grows ever clearer with each detail.

But the narrator, Ruth, opposes that process, telling us instead what Lucille is *not* doing, is *not* thinking, what she is *not* feeling, and in this way she offers us a vivid string of negative information, which cuts against the grain of a narrator's usual course of conversation with her reader. As a result, we envision, in sum, what is not happening, and we envision it powerfully, and this striking photographic negative causes us moments of some discomfort, while it also intensifies our engagement with the scene as we attempt to accommodate the contradictory sensation of seeing and hearing and feeling perfectly what is not there.

I should add that this reverse logic of language fits and amplifies the persistent thematic curiosity of the book itself: what loss or abandonment does to the one who's been left. Lucille cannot expel her sister, her family, from her memory, and hence their physical absence creates a searing presence, one that will always be in attendance.

So there is a certain readerly unease, an eager anxiety of sorts, created at the close of *Housekeeping*, as we are left feeling, not unfulfilled, but nevertheless that we, on our own, still have some work to do.

Alice Munro uses something of the same closing strategy to end her story "Fits," first discussed in the chapter "High Events." Her narrator, too, as we saw, diffuses the impact without diluting it in the least, by telling us what the protagonist, Peg, did not see:

> At noon, when the constable in the diner was giving his account, he had described how the force of the shot threw Walter Weeble backward. "It blasted him partways out of

the room. His head was laying out in the hall. What was left of it was laying out in the hall."

Not a leg. Not the indicative leg, whole and decent in its trousers, the shod foot. That was not what anybody turning at the top of the stairs would see and would have to step over, step through, in order to go into the bedroom and look at the rest of what was there.

The closing of "Fits," forgive the wordplay, doesn't neatly fit. Rather, it almost exactly straddles the line between summation and partiality. For though we do have a sense at the end that we have been given all the *information*—and so, from one standpoint feel the telling is complete—we are simultaneously left with the magnificent puzzle of Peg's behavior and its effect on her husband in their future life together, a future whose nature we cannot—and are not meant to—know at the point where Munro ends her story; or ends it, at least, insofar as there are no more words on the page. Which only makes for superb artistic balance, since, as noted in the earlier chapter, the high event of the story likewise takes place entirely off the page.

Flannery O'Connor, whose collected essays, *Mystery and Manners*, and letters, *The Habit of Being*, are brimming with practical insights into the art, addressed in other, and very helpful, language the issue of offering readers some departing summation. In a letter, dated May 4, 1955, to Ben Griffith, a writer and teacher and fellow Georgian, she wrote, "I frequently send my stories to Mrs. Tate [her close friend, the novelist, Caroline Gordon] and she is always telling me that the endings are too flat and that at the end I must gain some altitude and get a larger view."

That is a wonderful phrase, an ending needing to "gain some altitude," as it suggests the narrative consciousness lifting off at the end and looking down on the characters and events so that it can get some needed distance, see the forest of story and not just the trees, in order to make some definitive sense of things.

The first time I read this formulation of O'Connor's, via Caroline Gordon, I thought immediately of Joyce's ending of "The Dead," where the narrative leaves Gabriel Conroy's consciousness and rises lyrically, in the form of falling snow, into the white Dublin night and then continues on, above graveyards and open water until it is finally high enough to see first "the universe" and after that the landscape of immortality as well, the snow "faintly falling, like the descent of their last end, upon all the living and the dead." Altitude indeed.

In her letter, O'Connor was referring specifically to her story "The Artificial Nigger," which she had, typically, rewritten many times, finding particular frustration in trying to write an ending that satisfied her. She goes on to tell Griffith that "the end of "The Artificial Nigger" was a very definite attempt to do that [i.e., gain some altitude] and in those last two paragraphs I have practically gone from the Garden of Eden to the Gates of Paradise."

And so she did. At the close of the story, Mr. Head and Nelson, the grandson he is raising in the backwoods of Georgia, have returned home on the train from a day trip to Atlanta. In O'Connor's inimitable blending of comedy and schematic Christian rigor, theirs was an adventure hilarious to readers and harrowing for the participants, during which the hapless Mr. Head, a prideful fool, gets them lost while insisting he knows exactly where they are and in a moment of cowardly panic denies knowing his impudent young grandson, who, it seems, is about to be arrested for running into a woman and knocking her to the sidewalk.

Mr. Head's betrayal leaves Nelson stunned and furious, until his grandfather, finally undone by his shame and fear, sees a man walking his dogs and cries out, "I'm lost and can't

find my way and me and this boy have got to catch this train
. . . Oh hep me Gawd I'm lost!"

Told where they can board the train, the old man and Nelson head toward the nearby station, suddenly confronting on
their way a piece of racist statuary extending from the wall of a
wide suburban lawn. It is the encountering of this figure, "One
of his eyes entirely white and [holding] a piece of brown water-
melon," that mystically reunites, indeed spiritually fuses,
grandfather and grandson.

Here are the final two paragraphs, which O'Connor refers
to in her letter, describing Mr. Head and Nelson as they have
gotten off the train at their moonlit rural junction:

Mr. Head stood very still and felt the action of mercy touch
him again but this time he knew that there were no words
in the world that could name it. He understood that it grew
out of agony, which is not denied to any man and which is
given in strange ways to children. He understood it was all
a man could carry into death to give his Maker and he suddenly burned with shame that he had so little of it to take
with him. He stood appalled, judging himself with the thor-
oughness of God, while the action of mercy covered his
pride like a flame and consumed it. He had never thought
himself a great sinner before but he saw now that his true
depravity had been hidden from him lest it cause him
despair. He realized that he was forgiven for sins from the
beginning of time, when he had conceived in his own heart
the sin of Adam, until the present, when he denied poor
Nelson. He saw that no sin was too monstrous for him to
claim as his own, and since God loved in proportion as He
forgave, he felt ready at that instant to enter Paradise.

Nelson, composing his expression under the shadow of
his hat brim, watched him with a mixture of fatigue and
suspicion, but as the train glided past them and disappeared

like a frightened serpent into the woods, even his face
lightened and he muttered, "I'm glad I've went once, but
I'll never go back again!"

I do not need to describe the obvious overview presented
here, a consciousness that looks down from a virtually celestial
height. But, risking a kind of secular heresy, given the regard in
which O'Connor's work is deservedly held, I believe the closing of "The Artificial Nigger" and those of a few other of her
later stories suffer from having gained, in some sense, *too* high
an altitude. For me, the degree of explicit catechism in the first
of the two paragraphs of "The Artificial Nigger" suggests a
nearly transcribed Scripture, its tone verging on insistent
polemic.

O'Connor frequently described in correspondence her
annoyance at the critical ignorance and misinterpretation of
her work. In another letter in the volume, to her anonymous
friend "A.," she wrote, "Mr. Head is changed [by the action of
grace] even though he remains Mr. Head . . . Part of the
difficulty of all this is that you write for an audience who
doesn't know what grace is and don't [sic] recognize it when
they see it."

One gets the sense from her letters that the longer she
wrote in her tragically brief life the more irritated she became,
so the temptation toward increasingly unsubtle explanations
of her meanings is understandable, a conundrum every serious
writer is in sympathy with. Still, it seems to me that her frustration might have sometimes convinced her that she must
point too plainly to her thematic origins.

Having said that, I think the ending of "The Artificial Nigger" is rescued to a real degree by the last paragraph, where the
language returns very much to earth to complete its summarial
task, leaving readers with a ground-level picture of the newly
humbled Nelson and displaying all the sensory specificity that

O'Connor understood was the dusty work of writing and that she applied with her peculiar brilliance.

Partial Closings

I mentioned that the closing of summation, in its effort to tie things together, to culminate the story within its narrative confines, could be loosely equated to the fable's thorough opening, whose energy also resides within the "borders," beginning *with* and not before the reader's joining of the story.

In the same way, I would equate the more partial closing with those openings whose energy and action, as I said, suggest the story has begun *before* the reader joins it. A partial closing leaves a reader with the sense that the culmination occurs to a greater or lesser degree *after* the final period of the final sentence on the page.

Risking too sweeping a statement, it seems to me that the partial closing is more typically the province of the story, which, in contrast to the novel's span, delves for the relevant moment, the distillate fragment, although this represents an easily violated distinction, as we will see.

The challenge in writing a partial closing is in great part one of timing. Writers must have sufficient understanding of their stories' intentions and a sufficient feel for their rhythm and direction, so that they can guard against ending them prematurely. They must not, on the other hand, allow a story to continue on past the point of maximum impact—its drama having been played out, the effect like that of a stage curtain refusing to close, leaving the actors, their last lines spoken, to mill mutely about the stage.

The partial closing, in other words, should constitute a moment of earned surprise.

To this end, I have found it helpful to think of closing a story at its *penultimate*, rather than its ultimate moment. That is, if you as a writer have the requisite clarity for where your story is headed, and for how the forces and tensions you have put into play are ultimately going to collide, you might then cut the thread of your narrative at that point just *before* they do. At this juncture, the story should be carrying readers swiftly in a direction that seems more or less inevitable, and if it's ended right there, just as it's arriving, an effect is created that is at once satisfying—readers do not feel cheated or short-changed or that the writer has worked an unfair gimmick on them—and elliptical.

This is not a necessarily easy judgment to make, which is why I say a writer must, before he or she makes it, know fully where the story is headed and why it is headed there. It has been my experience, both as a writer, wrestling with my own unsatisfactory endings, and as a reader of new writing, that one often extends the telling of a story well past the point of its most powerful closing—takes it understandably enough to its ultimate gesture—and only sees on revision that the story could more impressively end some moments before that.

There are a generous handful of examples of such perfectly timed closings in Richard Bausch's collection *Spirits*, especially the story "What Feels Like the World," another depiction—by happy coincidence—of a day in the life of a grandfather and the young grandchild he is raising, though all similarity to "The Artificial Nigger" ends right there.

In Bausch's story, the granddaughter, Brenda, who is over-weight and clumsy, doggedly rehearses for an elementary school gymnastics demonstration to which all the families have been invited. She, alone among her fifth-grade class-mates, has been unable to perform the necessary vaults and jumps, and for all her practice and disciplined dieting it does not seem any likelier, on the day of the event, that she will be successful. Deep down, both Brenda and her grandfather feel this, and through conversations of brave encouragement and support and declarations that the whole thing is not important anyway there is a thickening air of doom as the hour approaches.

In the crowded gymnasium, the loving grandfather, sick with worry, waits and watches.

> The last of the sixth-graders goes over the horse, and Mr. Clayton [the physical education teacher] says into the microphone that the fifth-graders are next. It's Brenda who's next. She stands in the doorway, her cheeks flushed, her legs looking too heavy in the tights. She's rocking back and forth on the balls of her feet, getting ready. It grows quiet. Her arms swing slightly, back and forth, and now, for a moment, she's looking at the crowd, her face hiding whatever she's feeling. It's as if she were merely curious as to who is out there, but he knows she's looking for him, searching the crowd for her grandfather, who stands on his toes, unseen against the far wall, stands there thinking his heart might break, lifting his hand to wave.

And Bausch leaves the story there, at exactly the right place, the point of the reader's most intimate involvement. It is easy to imagine an untalented writer believing the scene should continue beyond this moment, so that readers would watch Brenda either miraculously making or failing to execute her jump. Both such endings would in opposite ways be equally horribly sappy. What helps to make Bausch's closing so effective is his understanding of a reader's human nature, which he legitimately manipulates to create a glorious tension at the end as we feel our sense of what is surely about to happen fighting, against all the evidence, with what we emotionally want to happen.

Finally, to show that the novel, also, can partially close and thereby confirm that my earlier statement was indeed too sweeping, I want to call back Alice McDermott's *That Night* one last time. We've already studied both its artful handling of the story's key dramatic incident and its instantly commanding opening. McDermott's gifts are obvious as well in the way she closes her story.

The narrative behavior of *That Night* is a wonder of leaps back and forth in time, a deliberate weave of speculation and reinvestigation that never leaves readers wondering where they are. This is an important factor in terms of its closing, for the book's final scene is not the story's last one chronologically. Instead, at the end, McDermott invites us again to be with her heroine, Sheryl, as she leaves the hospital after delivering her illegitimate baby and giving it up for adoption.

By this time the novel has shown us fragments of Sheryl's life long after the moment of the day on which it closes, and we've also spent a future hour with Rick, Sheryl's boyfriend and the baby's father, in his defeated adulthood some twenty years after that night. Consequently, with the narrative so segmented and directed this way and that, a strong underlying impression has been created that its completion will be in no way chronologically sequential. McDermott makes use of that license to end her novel. After paragraphs describing Sheryl before her pregnancy, impatiently counting the minutes at the dinner table until she can flee the house to be with Rick, and following the next paragraph, which refers once again to Sheryl's attempted suicide after she'd been whisked off to family in Ohio to have her baby away from the shame of local neighborhood inspection, we finally read:

In the front seat, Pam [Sheryl's earnestly well-meaning cousin], her mother and her aunt were keeping up a bright conversation to which the three children added their own bright and nonsensical things. Sheryl pulled her small cousin closer to her, held him more tightly in her arms. She tossed her hair back over her shoulder as Pam drove out onto the highway and the car picked up speed.

Some of what makes this ending seem partial, open-ended, is the image itself—the car accelerating, gaining speed as it drives away toward a destination not precisely described. Reading it, we feel the narrative circle *nearly* coming closed—in the way I described the effect of the ending of *Housekeeping*—but then, at the last moment, veering away from that point where the ends of the circle would touch and, as with the car, shifting into a faster gear, gaining a new, or renewed, power and continuing on into the American day. The visceral sense of this last passage is itself one of sudden redirection and acceleration.

After examining so many various endings for what makes each of them unique, it is important to close with an idea of what all good endings share. I said earlier in the chapter, in speaking of a particular closing, that what assured it its life, its resonant vitality, was that it left us as readers feeling that we still had some work to do.

Maybe that is it, the single factor that unites all successful closings—that they leave readers feeling they have some work still to do. More obviously, this quality could apply to those that end partially. But it might, just as much, characterize those of summation, with their patterned echoings and final connections that create new last sparks of current, like a web of hot wires touching everywhere.

If this idea is valid, then it should be quickly understood that the remaining work closings demand is not resented by readers. Not at all. Indeed it is work they are eager to do. Or at least that they are unable *not* to do.

Work they are unable not to do. Like writing.

8

Conclusion

In his 1961 Hopwood lecture at the University of Michigan, Saul Bellow said, "We have barely begun to comprehend what a human being is. . . . The novel . . . requires new ideas about humankind. These ideas in turn cannot live in themselves. Merely asserted, they show nothing but the good will of the author. They must therefore be discovered and not invented. We must see them in flesh and blood."

I offer this brief excerpt not merely for its refined intelligence, so characteristic of Bellow, or for its exhortative energy, welcome as that is, but primarily for the definition it contains of the fiction writer's mission—to give his or her "ideas about humankind" the incarnation of "flesh and blood." And furthermore, that these ideas can only have validity if they result, not from some bloodless abstract gamesmanship, from being merely "invented" in a rarified aesthetic laboratory, but from a committed and ongoing effort to "comprehend what a human being is."

As I understand Bellow's remarks, they seem among other things an endorsement of what is generally labeled realistic or conventional—as opposed to more experimental—fiction. Or, as I tend to think of one versus the other, fiction that seeks to comprehend and comment on life, versus fiction that seeks to comprehend and comment on fiction; and to emphasize in doing so that it is artifice.

Of course fiction is artifice. That's a given. But it seems to me more valuable—and even more demanding—to work to disguise that artifice and make it finally invisible than to perform all manner of linguistic flips and somersaults just to point it out.

So, underscoring what I hope has been apparent throughout, all the topics and discussions in this book—the drawing of complex characters; the peculiar logic and patterns of dialogue; the powerful indirection of dramatic events; et cetera— are most pertinent to an ambition to write realistic fiction. They derive from the great challenge to persuade a reader that the world on the page is the world. A world filled with people, causing and reacting to events, speaking to one another about the effect of those events.

Which is to say, stories. Artfully made, thematically rich stories. Stories inhabited by characters who are rendered so skillfully that a reader forgets, happily, edifyingly, that they are not real people. I have referred with admiration in these pages to the work of Wayne C. Booth, but there is one thing he says in *The Rhetoric of Fiction* that I reject. "Only immature readers," Booth writes," ever really identify with any character, losing all sense of distance and hence all chances of an artistic experience." Well, if this is the case, then I believe we should all aspire to be and, as writers, aspire to attract, wildly immature readers. I think the goal of the writer and the expectation of a reader should be exactly the wish to "lose all sense of distance" and fully "identify with a character." This seems fundamentally the example of the artistic experience—both in creating and receiving it.

I said in the introduction that for this book to be of use, a considerable demystification of the writing process was in order. And I said that the nature of the advice was highly practical, offered for the benefit of the committed craftsman. I hope all that has proven to be true. But now, having praised and promoted the idea of craft, I want to speak against it.

Having taught fiction writing workshops for many years, I have never been able to shed an underlying discomfort with certain aspects of the enterprise. As much as I believe in the worth of the strategies they can teach, and in the time they can save a new writer with talent who would otherwise be flailing about in trial-and-error frustration, I am always wary, and always will be, of a workshop's tendency to suggest that the solution to what is essentially wrong with a piece of writing can be found in craft.

But the true solution is never in craft. No amount of tweaking and altering—changing it from past tense to present; from first person to third—can rescue a piece of elementally flawed writing. While these recastings might indeed improve the work a bit, they will only postpone or defer the painful truth that a piece of fiction fails because it is ill-conceived or insufficiently inspired. Perhaps the ideas are skewed because the writer has not thought them through. Perhaps the characters are lifeless because the writer does not understand who they are. Perhaps the setting, the place, fails to invoke any sense of vital environment because the writer has never been there and cannot convincingly invent it from whole cloth. All of these problems confront a writer at various times, and none of them can be solved by altering an element of craft. They are too basic, too much matters of the writer's mind and heart and skill, and a change of voice or pronoun doesn't get us to any of those places.

And yet, again and again, I hear in workshops, someone asking, "What if I were to make the point of view a close third?" After which, in the spirit of democratic discussion, one ensues. A discussion, I hasten to point out, that I have too many times allowed.

This overly lenient workshop atmosphere reached its low point for me recently when someone in a workshop raised the issue of whether a story had a better chance, on one hand, of getting published or, on the other, being exposed as the submission of a sorry amateur, for having its length, its approximate number of words, indicated in the upper-right-hand corner of the title page. In response, virtually every member of the workshop jumped in, eagerly relating an experience or piece of advice he or she had received, one student referring the questioner to an article on the subject in a how-to-get-published magazine.

What was most regrettable, and my point here, about this ludicrous conversation was not so much the question and the spirited talk it provoked, but the fact that I, the incredulous teacher, allowed it to go on for maybe three or four minutes.

This is by way of saying that anyone who teaches aspiring fiction writers owes it to them to somehow make clear— within all the conversations about craft, all the discussions of point of view—the all too obvious truth that the one thing they must have in the end is the one thing no workshop can teach: a fictional imagination. In other words, talent.

But if a workshop cannot teach talent, it *can* teach, or at least promote, a certain frame of mind—a way of approaching the work that the writer and editor Ted Solotaroff, whom I have quoted elsewhere in these pages, calls "durability." In his essay "Writing in the Cold: The First Ten Years," Solotaroff writes that some of the most natural writers he has published over the years "are among the disappeared." And that "the decisive factor" in whether a writer will keep at it is not talent but "durability."

Durability. Doggedness. The daily habit of it. This is what

a workshop, with its emphasis on craft, *can* help to enforce, and it's a quality that's in real ways as necessary as talent if one is to achieve a sustained writing life. You may have talent. You may not. But if you do not develop a durability, an attitude that forbids you to tiptoe reverently around the work, you will really never know, and neither will anyone else.

The late Walker Percy wrote that one of the reasons he liked so much the small Louisiana town where he lived was because, as I remember the essay, he could sit in the local barber shop and the barber would ask a customer how his business, maybe the lumber business, was going. And the customer would say the lumber business was going all right. And when it was Percy's turn in the chair, the barber would ask, "How's the writing business going, Doc?" And Percy could say his business was going all right, too. That is, Percy's work was seen as having, in common with all other work in the town, the basic aspects of getting made and of then being released to a world of discriminating commerce.

But Percy did not mean "commerce" in anything like a narrow financial sense. And so, having advocated in the beginning that we strip away the mystery from writing, I want now, in the end, to restore it by emphasizing the necessary balance of gift and grit. As Percy implies, what is mystical about writing is the awarding of the talent—how much we are given; how little; if any. The possession of the gift itself is unarguably a spiritual transaction. While the rest of it, the daily business of craft, is bracingly pedestrian. It is with that luminous dailiness in mind that this book was written.

Works Cited
or Discussed

Austen, Jane. *Pride and Prejudice*. New York: Bantam Classics, 1984.

Bauer, Douglas. *Dexterity*. New York: Owl Books, 1999.

Bausch, Richard. "What Feels Like the World." In *Spirits*. New York: Linden Press, 1987.

Booth, Wayne C. *The Rhetoric of Fiction*. Chicago: University of Chicago Press, 1983.

Cheever, John. *The Wapshot Scandal*. New York: Vintage Books, 1992.

———. "The Cure." In *The Stories of John Cheever*. New York: Vintage Books, 2000.

Dickens, Charles. *Bleak House*. New York: Penguin Classics, 1997.

———. *Little Dorrit*. New York: Everyman's Library, 1999.

Dillard, Annie. "Notes for Young Writers." In *Image: A Journal of the Arts and Religion* 16 (Summer 1997).

Dostoevsky, Fydor. *The Brothers Karamazov*. New York: Bantam Classics, 1995.

Faulkner, William. *The Sound and the Fury*. New York: Vintage International, 1990.

Forster, E. M. *Aspects of the Novel*. New York: Harcourt Brace, 1985.

Fowles, John. *The French Lieutenant's Woman*. Boston: Back Bay Books, 1998.

———. *Wormholes*. New York: Henry Holt, 1998.

García Márquez, Gabriel. *Chronicle of a Death Foretold*. New York: Ballantine, 1988.

———. *One Hundred Years of Solitude*. New York: HarperPerennial, 1998.

Gardner, John. *The Art of Fiction*. New York: Vintage Books, 1991.

Gornick, Vivian. *The End of the Novel of Love*. Boston: Beacon Press, 1999.

Greene, Graham. *The End of the Affair*. New York: Penguin, 1999.

———. *This Gun for Hire*. New York: Viking, 1982.

Grimm, Jacob and William. "Faithful John." In *The Complete Brothers Grimm Fairy Tales*. New York: Grammercy Press, 1993.

Heller, Joseph. *Catch-22*. New York: Scribner, 1996.

Johnson, Denis. "Car Crash While Hitchhiking." In *Jesus' Son*. New York: HarperPerennial, 1993.

———. "Emergency." In *Jesus' Son*. New York: HarperPerennial, 1993.

Joyce, James. "The Dead." In *Dubliners*. New York: Vintage Books, 1993.

Kennedy, William. *Legs*. New York: Viking, 1983.

McDermott, Alice. *That Night*. New York: HarperPerennial, 1988.

Morrison, Toni. *Sula*. New York: Plume, 1982.

———. *The Bluest Eye*. New York: Plume, 1994.

Munro, Alice. "Fits." In *The Progress of Love*. New York: Knopf, 1986.

Naipaul, V. S. *A Bend in the River*. New York: Vintage Books, 1989.

O'Connor, Flannery. *Mystery and Manners: Occasional Prose*. New York: Noonday Press, 1969.

———. "The Artificial Nigger." In *The Collected Stories*. New York: Noonday Press, 1996.

———. *The Habit of Being*, edited by Sally Fitzgerald. New York: Noonday Press, 1988.

Orwell, George. "Reflections on Gandhi." In *A Collection of Essays*. New York: Harcourt Brace, 1990.

Oz, Amos. *The Story Begins*. New York: Harcourt Brace, 1999.

Robinson, Marilynne. *Housekeeping*. New York: Noonday Press, 1997.

Roth, Phillip. *Portnoy's Complaint*. New York: Vintage Books, 1994.

Said, Edward. *Beginnings: Intentions and Methods*. New York: Columbia University Press, 1987.

Shakespeare, William. *Richard III*. In *The Riverside Shakespeare*. Boston: Houghton Mifflin, 1974.

Smiley, Jane. *The Age of Grief*. New York: Fawcett, 1992.

Solotaroff, Ted. "Writing in the Cold: The First Ten Years." In *A Few Good Voices in My Head*. New York: Harper and Row, 1987.

Stowe, Harriet Beecher. *Uncle Tom's Cabin*. New York: Norton, 1994.

Tolstoy, Leo. *Anna Karenina*. New York: New American Library, 1988.

Updike, John. Introduction to *Loving, Living, Party Going: Three Novels of Henry Green*. New York: Penguin, 1978.

White, E. B. *Stuart Little*. New York: Harper Trophy, 1999.

Williams, Joy. In *Why I Write: Thoughts on the Craft of Fiction*, edited by Will Blythe. New York: Little, Brown, 1998.

Wilson, Edmund. *The American Earthquake*. New York: Da Capo Press, 1996.

DATE DUE
